HA HA AND AHA

THE ROLE OF HUMOR
IN PSYCHOTHERAPY

Harold H. Mosak, Ph.D.
Alfred Adler Institute of Chicago

 **ACCELERATED DEVELOPMENT INC.**
Publishers

Muncie,   Indiana

Ha Ha and Aha

The Role of Humor in Psychotherapy

Library of Congress Number: 87-70349

International Standard Book Number: 0-915202-65-4

Technical Development: Tanya Dalton
                            Judy McWilliams
                            Sheila Sheward

ACCELERATED DEVELOPMENT Inc., PUBLISHERS
3400 Kilgore Avenue, Muncie, IN 47304
(317) 284-7511

To My Major Teachers

Hedda Bolgar, Ph.D.
Roy Brener, Ph.D.
Andrew W. Brown, Ph.D.
Gilbert David, Ph.D.
Rudolf Dreikurs, M.D.
Elmer Friedman, M.D.
S. Thomas Friedman, Ph.D.
Erwin O. Krausz, M.D., Ph.D.
Walter A. Lurie, Ph.D.
E.H. Porter, Jr., Ph.D.
Carl Rogers, Ph.D.
Bernard H. Shulman, M.D.

Let reverence for one's teachers be equivalent to reverence for God.

Ethics of the Fathers, 4:12

The Talmudic sage, Rabbi Beroka, was accustomed to visiting the market place. One day, Elijah appeared to him. Rabbi Beroka asked the prophent, "Is there anyone in this market place who has a share in the world to come?" The prophet looked around and replied, "No."

While they were talking, two men passed by and Elijah suddenly said, "Wait, these men will have a share in Heaven." Rabbi Beroka then approached and asked them, "What is your occupation?" They explained, "We are jesters, and our job is to make men laugh, to cheer them up."

Treatise Ta'anit, p. 22a

PREFACE

What distinguishes people from other animals is said to be people's ability to laugh. If so, people spend considerable time distinguishing and differentiating themselves from the other members of the animal kingdom. Playwrights produce comedy. Comedians, standup and otherwise, tickle the funnybones of their audiences. Each year television bombards us with a new lineup of sitcoms. At parties, guests vie with each other in "Can you top this?" fashion to tell a better joke.

The general theorizing on humor is extensive, ranging back across the centuries through the philosophers, as well as more recently across the fields of anthropology, sociology, psychology, and psychiatry (Keith-Spiegel, 1972; Schmidt & Williams, 1971). Much of the literature treats humor as a "normal" but "pathological" phenomenon. We are told that humor is a form of regression in the service of the ego, that it conceals antisocial, sexual, and aggressive impulses. Some theorists frown upon its use in psychotherapy or advise extreme caution.

Hassett and Schwartz (1977) have observed that "Far more research has been devoted to the visual system of the frog than to what makes people laugh." While the total literature on the use of humor is relatively slight, the Adlerian literature on humor is miniscule but growing. This monograph provides a partial remedy for the situation. It first describes a theory which not only views humor as nonpathological, but as contributing to the evolution of social interest. It then describes the structure of the joke and proceeds to elaborate the forms and goals humor takes in psychotherapy, in keeping with Adler's dictum that in therapy a great advantage is when one is able "to keep the level of tension in the treatment as low as possible" (Adler, 1927b, p. 26).

My earliest academic training in psychotherapy was with Carl Rogers at the University of Chicago. Simultaneously I was serving an internship in a psychoanalytic setting. At the university I used "client" and at the hospital I had to use "patient." I now use them interchangeably, although one reflects my theoretical position and the other my medical model training.

The monograph originated with an address which I delivered to the Individual Psychology Association of Chicago many years ago. Jo-Anne Hahn converted it from spoken English to written English and added material based upon her special interests. Neal Mosak explained to his father the nature of children's humor, in which the structure of humor is more transparent than in adult humor, providing him with several insights into humor in general.

Harold H. Mosak

Harold H. Mosak
    Skokie, IL

CONTENTS

Part B. HUMOR IN PSYCHOTHERAPY

Part C. JOKES USED IN PSYCHOTHERAPY

Part A

HUMOR

Fun, Theories, and Structures

CHAPTER 1

WHAT MAKES THINGS FUNNY?

A jest's prosperity lies in the ear
Of him that hears it, never in the tongue
Of him that makes it.

—Shakespeare, *Love's Labour's Lost*

Reading about humor is somewhat similar to inviting a well-known comedian to dinner in hopes that he/she regale the other guests with witticisms. The great expectations with which the unwary are likely to approach either situation are almost certain to be dashed. Traditionally, nothing is unfunnier than the explaining of a joke, and writing about the origins and mechanisms of humor tends to convey a heaviness akin to the pall cast over a dinner party by the comedian who likes to save all of his jokes for the stage. Although notable exceptions can be found, some of the world's dullest and most abstruse papers are surely to be found focused upon the topic of wit and humor. This often ponderous empirical research and theorizing on humor is all the more strange if we consider the propensity of people to study and write on topics dear to their hearts, and the likelihood that authors of these studies consider themselves to have a sense of humor somewhat above that of the average wit.

While I cannot promise any greater levity than that provided by my more scholarly predecessors, if readers become desperate, they can turn for temporary relief to Chapter 6, which contains 150 jokes potentially useful in the practice of psychotherapy and in teaching about humor. Along with these are some that are just for fun. Meanwhile, the unfortunate experiences of the dinner host/hostess with the uncomical comic and of the neophyte student of wit can serve to direct our attention to some introductory observations on the question of what makes things funny?

Without question, expectation plays a part. Humorous content of the material would seem to be an obvious factor in bringing about laughter, but it is by no means essential. We approach a situation or an individual seen as potentially entertaining with a mind-set to laugh and enjoy. When a readiness to laugh is present, even the most minimal stimuli can spark it—most people, not only schoolgirls, laugh about "nothing." And when we have built up expectations to laugh, what Goldstein, Suls, and Anthony (1972) call "salience," we may experience disappointment and anger when these expectations are not met.

For most of us, we identify certain people in our lives as amusing or comical; these individuals arouse an anticipatory response in us and almost anything they say may be automatically laughed at. We know that certain professional comedians are "funny," and our expectations will be that they will make us laugh. "So-and-so really cracks me up!" A gesture, a phrase, a costume will set us up to laugh. We expect that other comedians will not, and we do not laugh. We make them work hard and often give them little reward in terms of laughter and applause. We may expect and are prepared to laugh at a night club but "Never on Sunday" in church.

Which of the comics among us has not had the puzzling but pleasurable experience of having even our most banal and inane remarks responded to with a barrage of laughter from those disposed to see us as funny? Incidentally, in this society, where having a good sense of humor is valued so highly that few people would admit to not having one (Treadwell, 1970), we gain an extreme gratification from being seen as the source of humor-arousal for others. Hence, when we encounter someone who enjoys our brand of humor, we are likely to find ourselves swelling up, rising to the occasion no matter what our previous mood, and becoming funnier in front of this receptive audience. Those who permit us to see ourselves as humorous are likely, in fact, to become among our most valued friends. (We tend to rate others as having a "good sense of humor" if they enjoy our jokes or find the same things funny that we do, i.e., a *good* sense of humor is *like mine*.)

In contrast to the natural wits, some of us seem forever doomed to be "straight people" for our more comic brothers/sisters. We are the ones who sometimes think of a superb *bon mot*—and *during* the occasion for once rather than as *l'esprit d'escalier*—but when we utter it to the assembled company, we find to our frustration that it falls, sometimes repeatedly, "flat as a pancake." A moment later our comic, who knows a good line when he/she hears it, picks up the remark, repeats it, and the company falls on the floor laughing at the previously ignored witticism.

If we laugh when we expect to be amused, as Shakespeare suggested, what about the person or the situation predisposes us to laugh? In addition to comic reputation, an empirically demonstrated influence on our readiness to laugh (Mettee, Hrelec, & Wilkins, 1971), the state of our interpersonal relations plays a part—we laugh at a joke when someone we like tells it. "Laughter at wit implies compliment," G. Stanley Hall and A. Allin (1897) observed, and, beyond friendship, may imply love, since "one of the earliest signs of love is sometimes the disposition to laugh at even the puerilities of the object of affection" (p. 29). As the popular song from *Oklahoma!* expressed it, "Don't laugh at my jokes too much; people will say we're in love."

True, we sometimes laugh "against our will." But that only demonstrates the potency of laughter and the fact that often a sense of power comes from getting others to laugh. One of the personality attributes of a joke-teller is that he/she is likely to be one who enjoys this sense of power. Perhaps this is why Mindess (Ansell, Mindess, Stern, & Stern, 1981) can make the statement that "My sense is that any therapist who uses humor in therapy likes to tell jokes and considers himself a funny person" (p. 19). Lenzberg (1937), noting that "wit may be used to strengthen a person's power," cited with some chagrin the case of students who "exhibit their witty repartee in a classroom demonstration and with it dominate the entire situation including the instructor" (p.

82). This power over others need not be exercised on the useless side of life through depreciating or hurting others, however. The therapist, for example, shares this enjoyment of power when he/she is able to turn the depressive around by making the client laugh[1] (See later).

Similarly, the joke-teller must be one who does not mind being the center of attention. The person need not be a chronic "attention-getter," but must be one who does not *mind* being in the spotlight. Often the person is one who actively enjoys being center-stage. In addition to a personality which enjoys attention and power, certainly the would-be comic could be helped by having some skill in the art of being amusing. At a minimum, a good joke-teller must have confidence in his/her ability to tell a joke. The person is *not* the one whose memory fails abruptly at the punchline or who says, "I can never remember jokes" (generally a self-fulfilling prophecy). A successful joke-teller has an implicit understanding of what is funny—which has nothing to do with knowing the theories of humor—and, in addition, knows how to tell a joke well. Some people have trained themselves lifelong to tell jokes, and they do it well out of accumulated experience.

Sometimes joking is a circular process in that the more the audience laughs, the more incentive for the joke-teller to continue. Often joking is a spiralling process in that the telling of a joke invites others to participate ("That reminds me of the one about..."). Sharing jokes and laughing together accomplishes two objectives—it serves as a social lubricant (Moody, 1978), and it enhances what Adler (1964b) called "social interest."

Professionals and amateurs may use different techniques to accomplish it, but both project an aura of funniness in order to arouse anticipatory responses in others (Lenzberg, 1937). Professional comics use posture, gait, clothing, accents, and props, as well as reputation, to create this readiness to laugh. In social situations, the wit may start off with a smile on his/her face or a characteristic twinkle of the eyes which

---

[1] That wit has considerable objective power as a social weapon has been demonstrated in the modern studies of humor as a "conflict-control" mechanism which functions either to "keep people in their place" or help them survive or escape from that place (Arnez & Anthony, 1968; Burma, 1946; Rinder, 1965; Stephenson, 1951); as well as in the changes wrought in history via satirists and caricaturists (Coser, 1959; Gray, 1966; Priest, 1966); and recently by the fact that several politically-oriented humorists achieved the high honor of inclusion on Nixon's "White House Enemies List."

proclaims, "Hey, I'm going to tell a joke," and people become prepared to laugh. The joke teller also may use certain opening cliches ("Have you heard the one about...?") to evoke the same anticipatory responses. This creates a preparatory mental set in the audience. These "play signals" (McGhee, 1979) invite the audience to adopt a laughing mood.

A good sense of timing is surely the most essential technique in successful joke-telling; timing involves reading the small cues from the audience, watching the build-up of their anticipatory expectations, maintaining their interest, and letting them hang, but not too long. A good sense of timing also means knowing how long to allow before starting the next joke, and how long to milk an old joke with creative new twists on it before going on to an entirely new line. While joking is *always* interpersonal (the only way you can tell yourself a joke and laugh is by imagining somebody else's response), timing is especially interpersonal, depending as it does on feedback from the audience, which is why reading a joke book or taping a joke session without an audience can be somewhat flat at best, and oftentimes notably unfunny.

Asimov (1971) added another variable in making a joke funny, cautioning and reassuring his readers that

> to be told effectively, a joke must be told well, and talents in that respect vary. In general, even those who tell jokes well are quite apt to find that their talent is not universal. ...If, then, you can't handle the necessary prose spontaneously, don't tell the joke. There are always many that will suit your particular bent, and since nobody is all-talented you need not feel cheated or deprived. (p. 3)

The audience composes still another major variable. Many avenues to that bit of knowledge exist. People speak of gallows humor (Freud, 1960; O'Connell, 1966), that "one does not joke about the gallows in the house of one who has been hanged." Professional comedians wince at appearing and perhaps "bombing" in front of a "tough audience" and delight in performing before an audience who, perhaps through anticipation, are convulsed with laughter even before the comedian has begun his/her monologue. Audiences who "sit on their hands" may create panic in the comic. The hostile audience provides a greater challenge yet with its "I paid my money. Let's see you make me laugh." The hostile audience may do such things as give away the punchline prematurely and destroy the "play signal" with "Not that old chestnut!" This audience behaves like a sulking child. While it refuses to laugh, it often can be cajoled into laughter, as Johnny Carson, for example, demonstrates on occasion. ("Come on, gang, I'm a veteran!") Other audiences are friendly, laugh easily, and even help the comic along by reciting the lines with the comic. Stereotypically some national groups are portrayed as easy laughers and others as laugh-resisters. The British are often depicted in movies as emitting a polite titter while the remainder of the audience may be rolling in the aisles.

Also to certain audiences we do not express humor or certain kinds of humor. Although with the advent of the women's movement circumstances are changing somewhat and some men feel free to tell risque jokes to some women, it is still considered in many circles inapropos to do so. Similarly a hush falls over the locker room when the clergyman enters after a round of golf. Adult joking also ceases amidst "sh-sh"ing when a child enters the room. In contrast, to some audiences we only tell certain jokes. These jokes, commonly referred to as "in-jokes" are understood by and intended to be understood by a restricted audience. "In-jokes" have been Bob Hope's forte. For nearly half a century Hope's peregrinations from one military base to another have been to present this form of humor—references to the military service, the base commander, Army food, and leering at women. To the extent that the non-military viewing audience shares the understanding, as for example the last mentioned topic, it may also share the laughter; other topics may leave the audience "cold."

Ethnic humor is often based upon the "in-joke." Others would not understand the joke unless it were explained, and when a joke is explained, it stops being funny. What complicates matters more is that certain ethnic concepts are not translatable into English. Examples of this are provided in the next chapter and others in Chapter 9.

One function that the "in-joke" performs is to create or reinforce a certain group cohesion or solidarity between the members of the "in" group, i.e., "Me and you are the same kind of guys, Archie." Thus, in ethnic humor we may tell jokes about ourselves that if "outsiders" told about us, we would find offensive. One Black may address another as "nigger" without any backlash. To call an adult Jew a "momzer" (bastard) constitutes provocation and invites retaliation; to call a Jewish youngster a "momzer" is a term of endearment characterizing the youngster as being cute and having a bit of the devil in him (Rosten, 1968). Similar "rules" apply to joke-telling. The same joke, depending upon who is the teller and who is the audience, may either be a funny "in-joke" or an offensive put-down. Lawyers hate the following story; others love it.

"A small boat capsized and a shark ate all the occupants but one. The survivor was a lawyer."

"Why didn't he eat the lawyer?"

"Professional courtesy."

Psychological factors such as the character and skill of the would-be humorist interweave with those of the listeners, with the context of the situation and the content of the humor, and all of these factors must be considered in any assessment of what tickles the funnybone and why. The boss' jokes, for example, are somehow funnier—at least we tend to laugh more readily and more heartily at them—than those told by someone below us in the status hierarchy. Other important *sociological factors* which influence our propensity to laugh include the size of the group (laughter in a crowd is more contagious than the Asian flu), the purpose of the group, and the age, sex, and status of those who comprise it or who constitute the target for laughter (Chapman, 1975; Dailey, 1966; Goodrich, 1954; Lundberg, 1969; Martineau, 1972; Murphy & Pollio, 1973; O'Connell, 1960; Wolff, Smith, & Murray, 1934; Young & Frye, 1966; Zijderveld, 1968; Zillmann & Cantor, 1972).

A few of these and other variables will be further touched upon in this section, but we do not intend to review the literature on humor. Such a survey would not be so much exhaustive as exhausting, since in addition to the scientific literature (Treadwell, 1967), a plethora of philosophers from Plato and Aristotle to Schopenhauer and Kant have written on wit and humor. An ungodly number of clergymen also have offered their observations and speculations on the topic,[2] as have numerous drama and literary critics (Fadiman, 1972) and even the comics and humorists themselves (Allen, 1972; Pirandello, 1965; Potter, 1951). Many of these offerings are repetitious, since most authors, like the present one, find reading their predecessors tedious, and after recapitulating a few major theories quickly abandon research citation in favor of expressing their own views. Here I will offer only a few gleanings from the general and scientific literature and will concentrate on the

---

[2]With apologies for the pun—which reminds us that the pun, as "the lowest form of humor," always requires forgiveness, but also that the apology functions as a means of directing the listener's attention to the pun, lest he/she overlook it—a danger only when the pun is a good bit more subtle and sophisticated than the present one.

Adlerian viewpoint. Chapters 4 and 5 of this book will focus on the use of humor in therapy, with particular emphasis on contrasting the Adlerian point of view with that of other approaches. The reader who is interested in becoming acquainted with Adlerian psychotherapy can find a description in Mosak (1984).

We must distinguish between joking, defined here as something said or done deliberately to cause laughter, and a sense of humor. A joke is always *made,* while the sense of humor is usually thought of as an attribute that someone *has* (Levine & Rakusin, 1959). The sense of humor encompasses the ability to amuse others and/or the readiness to laugh, both of which may or may not involve joking. Both joking and the sense of humor involve laughter, and we shall explore the interrelationships among the three.

We can begin by noting that while jokes and a sense of humor are always socially defined, laughter is most often both a physiological and a social event. Moody (1978) presented an extended description of these events. Occasionally laughter is almost purely a social event, as "polite laughter," which takes no more physiological involvement than is required for speech; at other times we experience laughter as primarily physiological, as in the "laughter of relief," but most often both aspects are interwoven. For example, although *funniness* is variously defined by different persons and is bound rather tightly by our memberships in various cultures or groups (Arnez & Anthony, 1968; Buckham, 1946; Dreikurs, 1951; Jason, 1967), a subjective evaluation that something is "funny" is nearly always accompanied by laughter or one of its variations, such as smiling or chuckling. Laughter, however, also may occur without humor, when nothing at all is funny in a situation. When it does, we generally call it "hysterical" or "bizarre," labels which imply disapproval and deviance from the social norms, thus reminding us that the physiological act of laughter is carefully regulated and controlled by society (Coser, 1959). Moody (1978) noted that "Ages ago, just as today, inappropriate or excessive laughter was regarded as a sign of madness" (p. 59). Such aberrant laughter is also symptomatic of physical disease, occurring in pseudobulbar palsy, amyotrophic lateral sclerosis, Nelson's disease, poisoning and intoxication, the pre-senile dementias, and multiple sclerosis (Moody, 1978). (This writer recalls the discomfort he felt 40 years ago when he, as an intern, was assigned a multiple sclerosis patient. Patient statements such as "I'm young and I'm dying and I don't want to die" were accompanied by outbursts of laughter.) In the psychological area hysterical laughter, hebephrenic laughter, and the lack of laughter in the depressed are labeled pathological. The lack of sense of humor in the paranoid and obsessive-compulsive patients is also well-known.

CHAPTER 2

THEORIES OF HUMOR

Humor falls into three broad categories—release-related theories, disparagement-related theories, and incongruity-related theories (Raskin, 1985). Others use such terms as "tension" theories, "put-down" theories, aggression theories, and "two-track" theories.

RELEASE-RELATED THEORIES

Our language gives us a clue to common folk beliefs about laughter as a primarily physiological-caused event. In milder forms of deviant laughter, we may experience ourselves as being "unable to contain" our laughter in a situation where its expression is not especially suitable, somewhat reminiscent of adolescent "giggling fits." When we talk about "uncontained" laughter that "bubbles over" or spills forth," we imply an energy force analogous to steam forcing the lid of the soup pot to rise, spilling its contents over the edges. Indeed, we use the very word "risibility" to express this almost involuntary inclination to laugh.

At times we intimate that laughter is expelled with the pent-up force of a volcano; it "erupts" and we "burst out" laughing or even "explode" with laughter. We are said to be "convulsed," to "bust a gut," or "split our sides" laughing, all phrases which contain the suggestion of laughter as the expression of a physiological "pressure." Freud (1960) has emphasized the primacy of this physiological view, hypothesizing that the strong driving forces behind the explosive release of laughter are innate sexual and aggressive drives, and that the function of laughter is to reduce harmlessly the tensions arising from these drives. We need not go along with Freud's theory of innate drives to recognize that humor certainly has a physiological component, but to limit our explanations to that narrow aspect of it is not necessary. While we have all experienced the subjective feeling of physical relaxation that follows in the wake of laughter, especially that of a hearty belly laugh, no clear empirical data exist on the extent to which laughter *per se* reduces tension. On the contrary, mirth appears to arouse and activate the sympathetic nervous system (Averill, 1969). We would suggest that the feeling of relaxed well-being may well be generated by the feeling of fellowship, that sense of belonging to the group and participating in it, which Alfred Adler (1963; Ansbacher & Ansbacher, 1956) called *Gemeinschaftsgefuhl,* rather than by any physiological drive reduction.[3]

We cannot agree with Koestler's (1980) view of laughter as "an activity devoid of any utilitarian value, quite unrelated to the struggle for survival...[which] has no apparent biological purpose" (p. 326). On the contrary, human beings appear to have been selected over the course of evolution for their expanding ability to laugh. Laughter, although it has what may appear to be an almost purely physiological or biological component, is essentially a *social* act which serves the evolutionary purpose of bonding. As we shall see later, *humor serves this purpose in bonding the relationship between therapist and patient.*

On the largely physiological side, perhaps, might be the laughter which we share with some other primates. Although laughter is often said to be uniquely human, Darwin (1965) long ago reported that other primates appear to "laugh" when please or tickled, and Van Lawick-Goodall's (1968) recent field observations confirmed that chimpanzees

---

[3]Maybe the Freudian language, with its concept of "storage" and "discharge" of "energy," is most at question (Young & Frye, 1966). Empirical studies attempting to prove analytical "repression of energy" theories have been generally inconclusive or controversial, at best (Berlyne, 1972). Nevertheless, clearly *something* physiological takes place, and we will continue in this paper to use Freudian language as a metaphor to describe the subjective feeling that the individual experiences of "building up" or "reducing tension."

laugh while at play, especially during violent tickling or wrestling. Such laughter, in chimpanzees and baboons in common with similar laughter in *homo sapiens,* seems to be an accompaniment of the physical and psychological pleasurable sensations which Darwin called "joy." Eibl-Eibesfeldt's (1970) accounts of the deaf-blind child who laughed heartily when she found her lost doll and who "laughed also when she danced while standing on her toes, which she had learned by herself," support the notion of laughter as an expression of the feeling of "joy." It feels *good* to be tickled, to be expending energy in the rough and tumble of play, or to achieve mastery over self or the environment, and so we laugh, chimpanzees, baboons, and humans alike.

At another physiological level Cousins (1979) described his recovery from a collagen disease in which his condition was considered to be hopeless. He discharged himself from the hospital and watched Candid Camera episodes and Marx Brothers movies which he maintains contributed to his recovery. His feeling was that if emotions could lead to disease, then perhaps "good" emotions could lead to recovery. He corroborated the Scriptural statement that "A merry heart doeth good like a medicine; but a broken spirit drieth the bones" (*Proverbs* 17:22). In agreement, Weinstein and Goodman (1980) observed that becoming more serious as we age "can be disastrous for our health" (p. 20).

Even in laughter which spills forth primarily as a physical expression of joy or pleasure, however, we can question whether or not a social or interpersonal element is present. Even if it were not present at the start, the interpersonal connection would inevitably follow the feeling of joy, because as Adler (1927b) pointed out, "Joy does not brook isolation." "Joy is indeed the correct expression for the overcoming of difficulties. It goes hand in hand with laughter in its freeing effect, representing the keystone of this emotion...It points beyond oneself and solicits the fellow feeling of the other person" (Ansbacher & Ansbacher, 1956, p. 228). A parallel to Adler's view may be discovered in Weinstein and Goodman (1980) who conclude that laughter is a natural state, that it facilitates connectedness and the feeling of belonging, and fosters a cooperative spirit.

The close interweaving of its biological and social aspects also can be seen when observing laughter in babies. Babies appear to laugh initially for the sheer joy of seeing or being in the presence of a loved one. The fact that children who are born blind and deaf initially laugh like normal children suggests the probability of an innate motor pattern, and, if so, it is one which performs the essential social function of cementing the parent-child bond (Freedman, 1964; Sroufe & Wunsch, 1972). In any case, what may begin as an innate motor pattern soon becomes enmeshed in the interpersonal web, and social feedback—or the lack of it—assumes primacy over any biological propensity.[4]

We would venture to suggest that laughter has a social or interpersonal aspect, even when seemingly indulged in alone. You can't tickle yourself or tell yourself a joke and make yourself laugh. When we laugh at the sight of our pets sprawled out in an awkward position, for instance, it is likely either the anthropomorphic nature of the position which strikes us as amusing or the anticipation of describing the scene to someone else which causes us to laugh. Similarly, the seemingly solitary laughter which occurs frequently in connection with dreams[5] or day fantasies involves an "imagined other," usually either as sharer of the laughter or as its target (and at the very least, in terms of the reference group from which the individual has taken his/her definition, of what is worthy of laughter) (Wieck, 1967).

In any event, so clearly is laughter understood to be a social act in this society that anyone who engages in it without an obvious "other" sharing it or causing it is considered eccentric or asocial at best. At worst, the person is considered to be in serious psychic difficulty, depending on how deviant his/her laughter is from the socially-set norms in terms of suitability of the amount of laughter and its intensity, as well as the appropriateness of time and place (Coser, 1959). One may not "howl" or "roar" with laughter, for example, unless sharing it with others who are doing the same. Nor may one refrain from joining in hearty laughter or substitute a titter for a belly laugh without considerable social wonderment and disapproval from the rest of those present. This social control exercised over our laughter has been empirically demonstrated in conformity studies (Nosanchuk & Lightstone, 1974). Laughter is contagious.

---

[4]Thus, blind infants who initially show the same smiling, laughing, crying, and expressions of anger, pouting, fear, and sadness as normal infants, soon decrease their smiling behavior as a result of lack of social feedback (Eibl-Eibesfeldt, 1970).

---

[5]There is a notion that people do not laugh in dreams which has been perpetuated in the scientific literature (Brody, 1950). It is not true; people often do and feel the same things as they do in waking life, and laughter is among the more frequent manifestations of emotions reported empirically in dreams, especially in the dreams of creative people (Adelson, 1974).

Laughter escalates as people top each other or even when they merely smile at each other in "schoolgirl giggles," although it has a tendency to shut down should a participant become too vulgar, too drunk, or both.

The overlapping or simultaneous physiological and social functions of humor also can be observed in action in a situation where sexual interests are aroused but where it is impractical to satisfy them: jokes, *double entendres,* and innuendoes which allow the release in laughter may be enjoyed by all participants in the situation. If we want to say something openly sexual, this might offend; it might offend our own ideals or it might offend other people. But through the medium of the joke we can still relax tensions harmlessly, without disrupting ongoing social relations. Men in our culture often use the joke as an "assessment technique" to determine whether they should go further in a seduction attempt. For example, a man at a party may pose this riddle:

"What is the different between a snake and a goose?"

"A snake is an asp in the grass..."

If the woman laughs, it opens up some further avenues; if she doesn't, no great harm has been done.

Freud (1960), in discussing the purpose of the smutty joke comments

> ...that smut is directed to a particular person, by whom one is sexually excited and who, on hearing it, is expected to become aware of the speaker's excitement and as a result to become sexually excited in turn. Instead of this excitement the other person may be led to feel shame and embarrassment, which is only a reaction against the excitement and, in a roundabout way, is an admission of it. Smut is thus originally directed towards women and may be equated with attempts at seduction. (p. 97)

Laughter, then, is for sharing. "Laugh and the world laughs with you..." Its evolutionary and adaptive function goes beyond the physical expression of joy and pleasure, of the reduction of tension to serve the essential social task of drawing those who share it closer together, whether they be infant and parent, members of a small group, working colleagues, therapist and patient, or strangers and brothers of the larger human community. Le Shan (1982) expressed a similar belief. Humor permits us to laugh at ourselves, it binds us to others. It makes life's problems easier to endure. It heals.

Humor is a clue that liking oneself is the beginning of being civilized to others. It is certainly important and difficult for parents to maintain a sense of humor about child raising. Laughter and humor helps us with all the frustrations, the impatience, that are a normal part of the human condition. Laughter is the greatest healer of all. When we feel depressed or tense, it may be because we have forgotten how to laugh... Laughter and humor are a necessary refreshment for the soul and sometimes the best way to deal with our problems. (p. 44)

DISPARAGEMENT-RELATED THEORIES

How can we reconcile the above view with that of the multitude of individuals who share Dryden's opinion of laughter as "Much malice mingled with a little wit?" The negative, destructive aspects of wit have been much more often observed, studied, and reported than the positive functions of joking and humor. According to Grotjahn (1966), who follows Freud, "wit begins with an intention to injure, which our culture requires us to repress..." (p. 14). In this view, when we have managed to repress our aggression, disguised it well, then permitted it to re-emerge as a joke or witticism, the pleasure that accompanies the release of the successfully-disguised hostility brings laughter in its wake. Some authors go so far as to insist that "There is inevitably a lubricant of hostility in all humor" and that "humor, by its very nature, is of the party of the opposition" (Rovit, 1967, pp. 242-243).

Freud's assertions about laughter and repression, though often repeated or elaborated upon and sometimes empirically tested (Baron & Bell, 1974; Berkowitz, 1970; Byrne, 1956; Dworkin & Efran, 1967; Keith-Spiegel, 1972; Kelling, 1971; O'Connell & Peterson, 1964; Roberts & Johnson, 1957; Williams & Cole, 1964) are by no means universally accepted (Berkowitz, 1970; Berlyne, 1972; Byrne, 1956; Goldstein et al., 1972; Leak, 1974; Ullman & Lim, 1962; Young & Frye, 1966). The findings that cartoons or jokes with sexual and aggressive content are judged to be more humorous than other jokes or that aggressive or angered people prefer hostile jokes, have been regarded as support for the theory of repression. Redlich, Levine, and Sohler (1951) are said to offer clinical evidence to support the Freudian hypothesis:

...one female subject who had explosive outbursts of temper consistently chose the most violently aggressive cartoons and gleefully identified herself with the aggressor in each case. She rejected with equal violence cartoons dealing with seduction and unattractive figures. She was found clinically to be sexually frigid and promiscuous and very much concerned about her sexual adequacy. (p. 724)

Similarly, Murray's findings that "subjects with strong, self-assertive trends who assume critical, hostile, and misanthropic attitudes toward their fellow men are those who most intensely enjoy disparaging jokes" are said to affirm the "intense laughter at derisive jokes is the consequence of repressed hate" (Redlich, Levine, & Sohler, 1951). A more parsimonious alternative offered by Byrne (1956) is that those subjects who express hostility are better able to recognize it in cartoons than those who do not express it. To Byrne, "the appreciation of hostile cartoons is seen simply as an expression of hostility by individuals who express hostility in other situations" (p. 87), a conclusion which fits well with the Adlerian view of the holistic and consistent nature of the life style.[6]

In this connection we can ponder the question raised by G.H. Mead (1934) of why we laugh at the man who stumbles and falls. It is almost *de rigeur* in writing on humor to advance one's own interpretation of the laughter that accompanies the "man who slips on a banana peel"—although Mead himself never mentioned the banana peel. Dreikurs (1951) suggested that the laughter is caused by the unexpected nature of the event, the surprise at the sudden fall. Others have interpreted it as relief at being spared the pain and embarrassment of having it happen to us (Roberts & Johnson, 1957). Most often offered are the *Schadenfreude* explanations which emphasize malicious enjoyment of others' misfortune. Rom (1971), for example, believed that people laugh at such an incident because "considering themselves in a position of superiority over the victim, they feel very happy indeed" (p. 227). In most such views, when we laugh when someone bends down and his pants split or when somebody falls down, we are expressing our own hostile feelings. We are said to be *glad* they're in trouble, *glad* that they're suffering, and that we look down on those poor dopes who have dumb things happening to them. From my point of view, this is not

---

[6]Similarly, recent researchers have demonstrated a positive relationships between the expressive behaviors of smiling and laughing in women and the evaluation of cartoon stimuli (Cupchik & Leventhal, 1974).

always so, although it is certainly true for some individuals.[7] The situation depends upon whether the viewer uses his/her feeling dysjunctively or conjunctively.

No rigid concept or explanation for the laughter in such a situation is needed. The sources of laughter are not mutually exclusive but can arise from more than one source simultaneously. Since some individuals may respond largely to one source of laughter and others to another, introspection contributes to the variety of explanations and to the certainty with which any one of them is asserted to be *the* true explanation. Our personal prejudice is for an explanation in keeping with Emerson's observation that ''The perception of the comic is a tie of sympathy with other men.'' That could be us falling there. That could be us splitting our pants in the street. We confirm for each other that we are human beings. While other primates share our psychological ability to laugh, only people can laugh at *themselves*. When we are laughing at others in this kind of predicament, we are basically laughing at our own humanness. ''There but for the grace of God go I.'' We are realizing our own humanness, our likeness to other people, our fellowship in the community of man, and our common vulnerability.

Disparagement takes other forms. Wolfe (1932) long ago called attention to what feminists are calling attention to today, that often ''The telling of smutty stories exemplifies the attempt of the discouraged to inflate their ego by the defamation of a member of the opposite sex'' (p. 186). It may often be a way of asserting or attempting to convince oneself and others that ''we're real men.'' This feminist view distorts what Wolfe actually said since he does not identify the sexes in the above statement. That this derogation can be bi-directional may be observed in Joke 100 in Chapter 9. However, erotically-tinged jokes may serve an entirely different purpose than expressing aggression. These jokes also have traditionally served the important social purpose of supplying clues as to whether a new romantic alliance may be arranged. The man may be indirectly announcing that he finds the woman attractive and she may indicate the degree of reciprocity by her laughter and response to the suggestive joke. Thus while a direct sexual approach by one person to

---

[7]Those who feel a strong sense of inadequacy and have a low self-esteem may be particularly susceptible to *Schadenfreude* humor (Mettee & Wilkins, 1972). Williams & Cole (1964) demonstrated that if persons are placed in a situation where they are made to feel inadequate, they will subsequently show an increase in their preference for jokes which depict the main subject as inadequate or in an ''ego-deflating'' situation.

another might be negatively received and cause a disruption in the previously harmonious relations between the two, phrased in the form of a joke, a covert sexual invitation can be met with laughter and interpersonal relations maintained whether or not the approach is fated to succeed or fail in its ultimate aim (Sykes, 1966; Zuk, 1966). In either case, laughter serves once again to maintain social bonds and increase social cohesion.

The jokes in the disparagement category, in addition to allowing us to express our aggression at those who place themselves above us, illustrate a point that Adler (Ansbacher & Ansbacher, 1964) made, that jokes often permit us to revolt against socially normal frames of reference. This feature of jokes struck Adler as most analogous to the neurosis. In both the joke and the neurosis, we find the striving for significance with tendencies towards the depreciation of others (Ansbacher & Ansbacher, 1956), and both the joke and the neuroses represent a revolt against the socially normal frame of reference. But whereas a joke can be good only if the two frames of reference appear to have approximately equal validity, Adler called the neurosis a "poor joke" because the neurotic has two frames of reference which are not equally valid. While the neurotic is familiar with the demands of normal community living, he/she does not meet them in common-sense fashion but operates by his/her own "private logic" (Dreikurs, 1974). The neurotic is characterized by a "yes-but" (two-track) movement in life.

The revolt against the customary social frame of reference was particularly important in the early days of psychoanalysis when Victorian mores were being overturned, and from that period we have the story, said to be true, about A.A. Brill. Brill, the reader may recall, went to Europe, studied with Freud, and then returned to the United States where he popularized Freudian theory. According to the story, he was giving a talk on psychoanalysis to a group of physicians and to the medical society in Boston. In the course of this speech, when talking about Freud's sex theories, the universality of sexual drives, and infantile sexuality, Brill mentioned parenthetically that just about everyone has masturbated at some time or another in his/her life. During the question period, one proper Bostonian physician arose and said, "Dr. Brill, I've listened to your lecture with great interest, but I want to take exception to one point, and that was the point about how common masturbation is. I'll have you know that I have never masturbated in my life!" Brill smiled at him and replied, "You don't know what you've missed."

Certainly, one of the purposes of laughter is to render dangerous people (e.g., Brill's critic) or institutions impotent. Another is to deflate people and institutions who are surrounded by or surround themselves with an aura of superiority; thus we have an abundance of jokes about lawyers, politicians, teachers, clergymen, doctors, psychologists, and psychiatrists. Clients will sometimes bring in "therapy jokes" such as the classic "can't win" complaint about the analyst that "If I come early to my session, you say I'm overanxious; if I come late, you say I'm resisting; and if I come on time, I'm compulsive!" Or psychiatrist jokes like the following:

> *Two men are walking toward each other on Michigan Avenue. They haven't seen one another for five years, and they start to pass. One man recognizes the other, stops and says, "Hello there, Dick!" but Dick merely calls out, "Hi, Tom," and continues dashing on by.*
>
> *Tom turns around, grabs Dick by the arm and says, "Hey, what's your big rush? I haven't seen you in five years. Stop and talk a while."*
>
> *Dick says breathlessly, "Well, gee, I'd really love to talk with you but I'm in a terrible hurry."*
>
> *"What's the big hurry?"*
>
> *"I have to go see my analyst down the street."*
>
> *"Well, okay, so you have to go see your analyst. Stop a minute and talk with me and you'll be a few minutes late."*
>
> *"Oh no, not me. If I come a few minutes late, the sonofabitch starts without me."*

The more hallowed or high status the institution and its agents, the more likely it is to become a favorite target for deflation by means of wit and humor, as in the joke about...

> *A priest and a rabbi sit next to each other on the plane as lunch, a ham sandwich, is being served. The priest turns to his fellow passenger and inquires, "Rabbi, why don't you eat your sandwich?"*

"You should know that we Jews don't eat pork products," *replies the rabbi.*

They continue to talk for awhile and now the rabbi asks the priest, "Father, have you ever had a woman?"

"You should know, Rabbi, that we priests are celibate. No, I've never had a woman."

"Better than ham, Father. Better than ham."

The aggressive element in these jokes may be seen partly as a rebellion against the control (or threat of it) which these social agents may exercise over our lives. It may also be an effort to "humanize" them, to bring them down to our level of common humanity from the rarefied atmosphere which some, at least, pretend to inhabit. (Or perhaps merely to knock them off the pedestal upon which we have first placed them.) The French novelist Stendhal (1924), according to Ellenberger (1970), was of the opinion that "The more we must respect someone, the readier we are to laugh at him" (p. 632). *Deliberate use of humor in therapy can serve the same function, to emphasize the humanness of the therapist and client,* as we shall see later.

Similarly, we laugh about death, a fact of life over which we have little or no control.

> Old man Mendel, on the point of death, is taking leave of his children, who are gathered about his bed. "Listen, children—all my life I have scrimped and slaved and have not permitted myself the slightest pleasure. I have always consoled myself with the thought that in the world beyond I should have nothing but pure joy. Wouldn't I laugh if there was nothing beyond!" (Lenzberg, 1937, p. 85)

Such jokes, as Lenzberg (1937) pointed out, make our suffering relative through embedding it in the suffering of all, and increase our strength by embedding that, too, in the strength of all.

In a near paraphrase of this joke, Lathrop (1981) commented,

> Oftentimes, the only humor in the accounts of unrelenting suffering to which I listen is the cosmic joke—the meaning of life is that there is no meaning. When I laugh at my own perpetual inclination to take myself seriously *and* when I can get the other to join me, there is a moment of relief from our existential aloneness. (p. 9)

INCONGRUITY-RELATED THEORIES

Laughter from jokes need not be pegged *either* physiological or social; it is both. It is also simultaneously and inevitably cognitive. Adler emphasized the cognitive aspect of jokes. We don't laugh at a joke unless we understand it, and that requires mental processes sufficiently well-developed and mature enough (Graham, 1958; McGhee, 1972a, 1972b) to perceive incongruities and to reconcile them (or to laugh at the gap remaining after the irreconcilability becomes evident, as in shaggy dog stories). Adler (1972b) asserted that two frames of reference are always present in a joke. The joke is funny because the teller leads the listener in one direction and then trips him/her up with the punchline because it shifts direction in a way other than the one expected. The listener becomes so wound up going down one path that when the punchline comes, he/she wonders, "Where did that *one* sneak out from?" It has a different meaning from the one already attached to it, as in the story of...

> ...the obsessive-compulsive who goes to his therapist every week and complains, "Gee, Doctor, I have this terrible urge. I don't know what I'm going to do about it. You know, every time I go into the delicatessen on the corner. I have this terrible urge. I can hardly control it. I want to stick my penis in the pickle slicer."
>
> The doctor tries to analyze the urge, but he doesn't get far with that. The man merely repeats, "I feel this urge."
>
> Each week he returns and says, "It's getting worse. It's getting more intense; if something isn't done about it soon, I don't know what's going to happen."
>
> And finally, as the doctor is becoming more and more alarmed, the patient comes in one day and, with a big smile on his face, announces, "Doctor, I did it! I did it, I **did** it, I DID it! I stuck my penis in the pickle slicer."
>
> And the doctor says, "My God! What are you so happy about?"
>
> To which the patient replies, "Why not? She finally let me!"

In the Freudian view, this joke would be funny because it reduces tension; we think that it is more likely to raise the level of tension. Actually, it appears to be that the most successful jokes first raise the level of tension somewhat—but not too high—and then relax it (Berlyne, 1972; Kuhlman, 1984; Levine & Abelson, 1959; Levine & Redlich, 1960). Simultaneously and more importantly, the laughter comes about from the surprise switch of tracks; without our cognitive (if subliminal) awareness, no tension would be built up nor any release through recognition and reconciliation of the incongruity of two divergent lines of thinking.

In any case, every joke has two frames of reference, and the more successful the joke, the more likely the frames of reference are equally valid, as in the joke about...

> ...the interracial cemetery in San Francisco where a Caucasian man is pulling weeds and puttering around the grave of one of his family. He very lovingly places flowers on the grave, and when he looks up, he sees an Oriental man at the next grave placing a bowl of rice lovingly on the grave of one of his family. The Caucasian man laughs and inquires, "Hey, who's coming up to eat your rice?"
>
> The other one smiles benignly and replies, "The same one who's coming up to smell your flowers."

At the same time, in the Adlerian view, humor always involves some kind of incongruity. It may be an exaggeration, a contradiction, an understatement, a reversal, a surprise, something ludicrous or totally unreal, but humor always involves some kind of cognitive discrepancy. (See Chapters 3 and 9 for further examples.) Asimov (1971) concurred, writing "that the one necessary ingredient in every successful joke is a sudden alteration in point of view" (p. 1).

On the simplest level of cognitive discrepancy is the pun or joke which plays on two meanings for the same word or sounds or treats something literally which should not be understood literally. In the first category is this joke from the old Henry Morgan program where the "professor" was playing an authority on etiquette. The straight man inquired of him, "Professor von Morgan, should olives be eaten with the fingers?" and von Morgan replied, "No, the fingers should be eaten separately." One reason why puns often elicit a pained "ooof" or groan from the audience and are nearly always followed by an apology is that they seldom present equally valid frames of reference. (In fact, a correlation may be between the length or anguish of the groan and the amount of stretching the "equal validity" of the second frame of reference in the pun.)

Similarly, the famous story about Harry Hershfield is told,

> *A gentleman who had eaten too well at a formal dinner and suddenly felt an overpowering urge to belch. Unable to hold back, he emitted a loud belch. This left the stuffy gentleman across the table outraged, and he demanded, "Sir, how dare you belch before my wife?"*
>
> *Apologetically the culprit replied, "Gee, I'm sorry. I didn't know she had first turn."*[8]

Burns and Allen used this form in signing off their comedy show.

> *Burns: "Say good night, Gracie."*
>
> *Allen: "Good night, Gracie."*

Children do it this way:

> *Tom: My friend, Mary, can spell any word in the English language.*
>
> *Bob: I don't believe it. I'll bet she can't spell antidisestablishmentarianism.*
>
> *Tom: Okay, Mary. Antidisestablishmentarianism. Spell it.*
>
> *Mary: I-T.*

---

[8]In the novel, *Fine,* Shem (1985) tells the story this way:

> Staggered by V's intuitive brilliance, Fine confessed his fart. To his surprise, V told a joke which ended:
>
>> ...and so Tausk turned to Freud and said, "You farted before Lou Andreas-Salome!"
>>
>> And Freud said: "Ah, and was it her turn?" (p. 146)

CHAPTER 3

THE STRUCTURE OF THE JOKE

When examining the structure of a joke, one learns more from co-medians discussing the matter on TV talk shows than one does from the psychological literature. In the latter, the pioneering work is Freud's *Jokes and Their Relation to the Unconscious* (1960) in which he understands jokes to be funny because they are expressed in the language of the primary process. Primary process language may be represented by the form of thinking which goes on in dreams. It relates a story but in a different language than the one we customarily employ in our waking state. It is the language of symbolism, the "forgotten language" of which Fromm (1951) spoke. As with any language, it possesses its unique grammar.

The thinking of the young child occurs in primary process language, and Freud offers the theory that jokes are funny because they permit us to regress to an infantile manner of thinking. Instinctually we require certain kinds of gratification, especially of our sexual and aggressive in-stincts, and the joke, through primary process language, permits it. Humor, said Brenner (1955), is a vehicle for regression in the service of the ego and therefore nonpathological. Take the joke about...

> *...the nice old Quaker lady who was driving down the street. She came to a red light, and being a law-abiding citizen, she halted her Volkswagen. Right behind her a man was driving a large truck. Since he was very busy ogling the girls, he didn't notice that the light had changed, and he rammed into the rear of the Volkswagen. When the dust had settled, the old Quaker lady emerged from the car, brushed the dust off her clothes, and walked back to the truck. She looked up and with a serene expression on her face, told the truck driver, "When thee gets back to thy kennel tonight, I hope thy mother bites thee."*

If we were to phrase the punchline in secondary process (conscious, non-symbolic) language, it becomes "you son of a bitch" and the humor disappears.

Since Adlerians reject the importance or even the existence of an instinctual life, Freud's theory of wit finds unacceptance, and we must substitute an instinct-less and ego-less theory in explanation. For the Adlerian, humor must always involve some incongruity—a contradiction, a surprise, something ludicrous, a double meaning. In children's humor we can see this two-track phenomenon in its baldest form:

> *You are the conductor of a train going from Chicago to New York. You leave Chicago with 75 passengers. In Cleveland 18 passengers board and 23 get off. At the next stop, Buffalo, 37 passengers exit and 21 board. Then the train stops in Albany where 13 passengers get on and 27 get off. The next morning the train arrives in New York City. How old is the conductor?*

[There *is* an answer. Look back at the first sentence.] Joke No. 123 (Chapter 9) is an adult version of the same type of two-tracked joke.

JOKE CATEGORIES

If one investigates humor, one can observe families of jokes. With respect to content, one often hears the comment that jokes can be classified into ten (or some other small number) original or basic jokes and that all other jokes are derived from them or variations upon them. Similarly in terms of process, jokes can be classified within a small number of families.

1. The Double Meaning

In children's humor, a joke often finds expression in finger games. A child holds up two fingers in "V for Victory" or "Peace" sign and asks, "What is that?" After permitting you to make the conventional guesses, he/she gives you the "right" answer: "It's a Roman ordering five beers."

Again from children's humor: "If Congress passed a law that all automobiles had to be painted pink, what would we have?" Answer: "A pink carnation." Jokes Nos. 16, 33, and 35 are adult examples, as are puns and *double entendres*. At a more complex level, the story is told of...

> ...the two hunters, one smart and one dumb, who went out for a day of shooting in the woods. Deep in the woods, they came to a clearing in which stood a small cottage. Out of the house came a gorgeous woman in the nude. The smart one ran up to her, embraced her and inquired, "Are you game?" When she nodded, the dumb one raised his gun and shot her.

2. The Surprise

In this form the punch line sneaks up on you, and you feel "I'd never in a thousand years have expected that." Jokes 54, 60, 62, and 79 are illustrative. And take Myron Cohen's joke:

> Diner: "What's that fly doing in my soup?"
>
> Waiter: "Looks like the backstroke to me."

3. The Reversal

These jokes are funny because they demonstrate incongruity through reversal (Cf. Asimov, 1971, p. 4). Children form this kind of joke as follows:

> "What do you get if you cross an elephant with peanut butter?"
>
> "You get either a peanut butter with a long memory or an elephant that sticks to the roof of your mouth."

An adult version goes like this:

> *A man is teaching his son how to fly a kite but he can't get it off the ground. A sympathetic neighbor comes over and offers his assistance, but without better success. The first man's wife is standing on the porch unable to contain her amusement with the proceedings. Her husband, frustrated by his lack of success and irritated at her amusement, turns and demands, "What the hell do you think is so funny?"*

> *She responds, "No wonder it's not flying. What you need is more tail."*

> *Shaking his head in disgust and anger, he turns to his neighbor and exclaims, "Sure, and when I tell her I want more tail, she tells me to go fly a kite."*

Jokes 25, 32, 74, 78, and 88 are additional illustrations.

4. The Contradiction

These stories have their effect because the joke possesses an internal contradiction. Thus Groucho Marx's rejection of an invitation to join a country club: "I wouldn't belong to any club that would have me for a member." Or, "What would you do if you found a thousand dollar bill on the street?" "Well, if it belonged to a poor man, I'd return it."

George Burns (Carter & Greenberg, 1976) explained the process:

If a joke has a funny foundation and an honest premise, it can live forever. Like the time Gracie put the salt in the pepper shaker and the pepper in the salt shaker. I said, "Gracie, why do you do that?" and she said, "Because people are always getting mixed up and now when they get mixed up, they're right."

We call it illogical logic.

5. The Ludicrous Story

This story is incongruous because it is exaggerated, out of proportion, or even out of this world. In some manner it is on a different track from realistic expectation. Some could not occur even in the wildest imagination. A child might ask:

"How do you get five elephants into a Volkswagen?"

*"I don't know. How **do** you get five elephants into a Volkswagen?"*

"Simple. Three in back and two in front."

Or, Myron Cohen in his airlines commercial tells of the nice, elderly Jewish man in Brooklyn who calls the reservations office and inquires,

"Do you fly to Miami?"

"Yes, we do."

"How long does it take?"

"Just a minute..."

"Thanks very much."

Or,

> *Three women are sitting at the beach comparing their lives. The first says, "My husband who's in transportation, such a rich man, sends me here every winter for three weeks."*
>
> *The second woman, anxious to demonstrate her superiority, says, "My husband is a CPA and every winter he sends me here for the whole winter."*
>
> *The third woman says, "Well, I'm happy for you both. My husband is a factory worker. I'm lucky to get a week down here every few years. But he has a penis so long that twelve pigeons can stand on it side by side."*
>
> *"Oh, come on," says the first woman. "Who are we kidding? Sure my husband is in transportation. He's a taxi driver."*
>
> *"Okay," says the second woman. "If we're going to tell the truth, I'll have to confess that my husband's not a CPA. He's a bookkeeper."*

> *"All right," says the third. "I'll stop exaggerating also and tell the truth. It is true that twelve pigeons can stand on his penis, but the last one has to stand on one foot."*

Other examples of the ludicrous story may be found in Jokes Nos. 36, 85, 96, 99, and 104.

6. The "Nothing Sacred" Joke

In 1927 Adler wrote an article in which he observed that many jokes permit a person to revolt against a socially normal frame of reference (See Chapter 1). Irreverence, satire, and lampooning are characteristic of this form. Everyone and everything is fair game, and we have jokes about psychiatrists, clergymen, ethnic groups, sick jokes, gallows humor, and our most hallowed institutions. While many of these jokes superficially seem to be derogatory, their purpose often is to humanize rather than degrade the "sacred." There is the story of...

> *...the Virgin Mary, who was interviewed by a reporter.*
>
> *"How do you feel about being the Mother of Jesus?"*
>
> *"To tell you the truth, I was hoping for a girl."*

Jokes Nos. 101 and 105 do it to Adlerians and Rogerians respectively.

However, many of these jokes are designed to buy superiority at the expense of others. Some of these would be structurally funny if they were not ethnic. Fill in your own choice of ethnic group in the following joke.

> *"What are 1492 and 1776?"*
>
> *"Connecting rooms at the Slobbovian⁹ Hilton."*

Other jokes in this group are insensitive and often verge on the hurtful and cruel. Only an "in-group" of people who like to put down other people find them funny. Members of the offended group find no humor

---

⁹When I was first told this joke, it was at the Warsaw Hilton, but one can insert the name of any ethnic group's country the teller may wish to deride. There is no intention upon my part to in any way deride the Hilton hotels at which I have often enjoyed staying.

in these jokes. One major exception exists according to Mindess (Ansell, Mindess, Stern, & Stern, 1981) and Kuhlman (1984). People within an ethnic or religious group can tell the very same stories to other members of their group with resulting hilarity. The phenomenon is parallel to the older brother who beats up his sister but will beat up anyone else who tries to beat her up.

7. Laughing at Oneself (Self-Disparagement) Humor

Jimmy Durante and Bob Hope laughed at their noses, Jack Benny at his stinginess, and Rodney Dangerfield complains, "I don't get no respect." "If it rained borscht," Milton Berle gloomily observed, "I'd be caught with a fork." Much Jewish humor falls within the category and has been explained as a survival mechanism. Rabbi Ben Ezra, whom Robert Browning memorialized in a poem, in a verse of his own wrote,

> *"If I sold lamps,*
> *The sun,*
> *in spite,*
> *Would shine at night."*

Jokes Nos. 72 and 76, when told by a psychologist, fall in this group.

Rule (1977) has experimented with this form of humor which apparently leads to increased self-and other-acceptance.

Self-disparagement humor also can serve the purposes of (1) beating other people to the punch and (2) obtaining extra attention.

8. The In-Joke

The in-joke is one which the "in" people will understand and laugh at. Giving an example of such a joke poses problems because some readers may be "in" people with respect to the joke and some "out." If you are a Chicagoan or follow baseball, you may enjoy the following riddle:

> *"What has 18 legs and lives in the cellar?"*

> *"The Chicago Cubs."*

In-jokes, Martineau (1972) explained, reinforce in-group alliance and elevates its morale.

Much ethnic and religious humor falls into this category (Rosten, 1968). Unless you are familiar with the Jewish laws regarding *Kashruth,* the following joke will be meaningless. To those who are "in," the joke produces a "belly-laugh."

> *Mendel, having developed a rash on his penis, consulted his doctor who told him to soak it in hot water. Fearful of his wife's learning of his affliction, he took a pot from the pantry, filled it with hot water and went into the bathroom to soak. However, he forgot to lock the door, and his wife, Gitel, walked in. Mendel, caught unaware, sputtered a defensive remark, "I have a rash, and the doctor told me to do this."*

> *"Rash-smash, get your meat out of the dairy pot!"*

9. Black Humor

These deal with the tragic (Asimov, 1971). "Where an anticlimatic incongruity becomes sufficiently sharp, when, in particular, it is something as serious as death that is downgraded by another's mere inconvenience—we have an example of...black humor" (p. 6). We feel we shouldn't laugh at the joke, but "It is precisely the fact that we laugh that demonstrates our humanity" (p. 6).

> *These four golf nuts never let anything interfere with their playing a round of golf. This day they're out on the golf course, and as one of the golfers is about to tee off, a funeral procession passes by. The golfer stops for a moment, removes his cap, and places it over his heart, and as he is lining up the ball, dolefully informs the other members of the foursome, "Yes, we would have been married 35 years today."*

10. Sick Humor

Moody (1978) wrote, "In the late 1950's the term 'sick joke' was coined to denote a variety of humor...which one feels, would only be thought funny by someone who was emotionally disturbed—who was, to be more specific, sadistic" (p. 60).

"Why did the vain woman refuse to have a colostomy?"

"Because she couldn't get shoes to match."

Readers of *Hustler* will recognize this genre.

11. Gallows Humor

Freud (1960) described this as "the crudest form of humour" and illustrated with

A rogue who was being led out to execution on a Monday remarked: "Well, this week's beginning nicely" (p. 229).

An Adlerian who has studied this form of humor extensively, W.E. O'Connell, has reported his findings in several places (Cf. O'Connell, 1966).

12. Topical Humor

Also discussed by Freud, this type of humor is funny by construction but is only funny at a specific period of time. Much political humor falls within this category. Franklin D. Roosevelt was the only American president elected four terms. Before the 1948 elections the Democrats, many of them opposed to slating Harry S. Truman, were searching about for a candidate. The story had it that in 1948

> *...a Democrat and a Republican were talking about their respective parties' nominees. The Republican said, "It looks like we're going to go with Tom Dewey. Who are you Democrats going to run?"*

> *"I don't know but we'll dig someone up."*

> *"No, not* **him***!"*

A very funny joke in 1948; today, many people would be hard put to remember the characters, much less think the joke funny.

Just as probably more than ten basic stories exist in terms of content, undoubtedly more than twelve categories exist. However many there may be, they all nevertheless display the two-track phenomenon.

Part B

HUMOR

IN

PSYCHOTHERAPY

CHAPTER

ROLE OF HUMOR
IN PSYCHOTHERAPY

*Jesting often cuts hard knots
more forcefully and effectively
than gravity.*

—Horace, *Satires* I. x. 14-15

Dialogue by professionals who debate the use of humor in therapy often seems to be going in opposite directions; not much common ground is in their basic assumptions, and, like the previously cited olives and fingers pun, their remarks tend to slide past one another without ever meeting.

Laughter in the traditional psychoanalytic hour is often regarded as pathological, a "sign of foreboding," or at least as highly undesirable (Brody, 1950; Kubie, 1971; Marcus, 1969). Kubie (1971), perhaps the major spokesman against the use of humor in therapy, generally foretold doom and disaster if humor should be indulged in by client or therapist in the psychoanalytic hour. He believed that humor in therapy is entertaining and amusing for therapists and contributes to the enjoyment of their work, but is detrimental for the client, whereas Adler (1927b) felt, "I have always considered it a great advantage to keep the level of tension in the treatment as low as possible and I have virtually developed it into a method to tell almost every patient that there are jokes like the structure of his particular neurosis, and that therefore one can also take the latter more lightly than he does" (p. 26).

Because of Adler's emphasis upon the therapeutic use of humor, he (1973) felt that in addition to their specific training, therapists also should possess "sagacity and ingenuity, a jovial attitude...blessed with cheerfulness and good humour...also extreme patience and forbearance" (p. 201).

We believe with Adler that humor is valuable and therapeutic, and in this section will present our view of some of its benefits in psychotherapy.

ROLE OF HUMOR IN ESTABLISHING
A RELATIONSHIP

> *Humor is Emerson's "merry sphinx," custodian of hidden wisdom, guardian and restorer of sanity...It creates a tie of mystical fellowship passing swiftly from mind to mind, and heart to heart, like a gleam of sunshine through a winter wood.*
>
> —John Wright Buckham

Those of a "humanist" persuasion who believe in relating person-to-person in a genuine, warm, human way with the client find it difficult to believe that others still can talk about the "necessary incognito" of the therapist (Kubie, 1971). New therapists trained in the "neutral" mode of relating too often seem to have to discover for themselves that humanity and sharing of one's self is therapeutic. They come to that knowledge slowly and tortuously through long experience, accidentally hitting upon it by trial and error, and usually when all else has failed. Marcus, for example in a long article in 1969, after affirming Brody's (1950) observation that laughter and smiling are not common in analysis and when present, are better left undisturbed, then somewhat hesitantly offered anecdotal evidence which evidently surprised him, that smiling appropriately at a critical moment in therapy helped a patient. He tentatively concluded that his unneutral smile, while perhaps "of minor significance or contraindicated when working with healthier individuals," did seem to mark the turning point for a severely regressed patient.

For Brody to have reported that "Laughter is not common during the analytic hour" (p. 192) is not strange because he also asserted that "As a rule it is the sickest types of personalities (the schizophrenic, the schizoid, or the compulsive) who laugh or smile frequently during the analytic session" (p. 192). Clients sensitive to what is happening in interpersonal transactions would rapidly catch on to this attitude and control their tendencies to be humorous. If not, they would quite likely have their humor analyzed, with almost inevitable confirmation of the therapist assumptions that "the superficial cloud of mirth that cloaks it is all too easily dissipated, leaving a substance of sadness, despair, regret, anger, or hatred that may overwhelm the patient" (p. 193). Brody went on to state:

> This we found true in nearly every instance where we persisted in attempting to analyze our patient's laughter. In most instances the meaning of the laughter arose from such deep sources of the unconscious and was so far removed from the patient's understanding that it was futile to continue its pursuit. (p. 193)

If his/her early humor attempts are met with such scrutiny and chronic pessimism, it is small wonder that "the patient becomes uneasy, fearing he is being laughed at or accused of having laughed at the analyst" (Brody, 1950, pp. 192-193). In our view, the underlying "substance of sadness, despair, regret, anger or hatred" that such analysis of laughter "uncovers" might well be a *normal* reaction to being misunderstood and covertly told that you are not healthy enough yet to be permitted to enjoy life, the increased understanding of one's self, the sudden glimpses into the paradoxes of one's thinking that laughter in therapy often signals.

The client's anticipation of the therapist's negative response to his/her sense of humor could be one factor in the compartmentalization reported by another analyst:

> In some obsessional patients, in my experience, a well-developed sense of the comic is isolated from the analytic situation by being expressed only in the social life of the patient. It is with some surprise that the analyst discovers that such serious, dour patients are regarded by their friends as "lives of the party" and unusually "funny fellows." (Rosen, 1963, p. 720)

Such clients may be healthy enough to use their humor only where it is welcomed and appreciated.

Interestingly enough, even the psychoanalysts are willing to permit and sometimes encourage laughter and humor "towards the end of therapy." We can wonder if by inhibiting the client's earlier use of humor they are not arbitrarily prolonging the therapy until *they* decide that the client is "healthy enough" to get even healthier.

Kubie (1971) considered the authoritarian-expert role for the therapist to be inevitably thrust upon the therapist by the client—and it doubtlessly is under traditional psychoanalytic conditions. But it need not be so. *Adlerian theory not only permits but encourages the therapist to be "human," to be a fellowman to the individual he/she is trying to help. The client is not in a submissive position vis-a-vis the "expert"* (Mosak & Phillips, 1980), *but the two of them make a contract to work together in an atmosphere of mutual respect, as fellowmen* (Mosak, 1984). *The low level of tension facilitates such a cooperative task-solving approach.* Adlerians view therapy as an educational and re-educational process, and believe that learning occurs more readily in a relaxed atmosphere.

Sharing and caring go hand-in-hand in Adlerian psychology. Humor may accelerate the attainment of these goals in that humor permits bonding and connectedness both in and out of therapy. Narboe (1981) described it well. One of her "gut" indicators

> ...that therapy has indeed begun—whether during an initial meeting or in the second year—is humor. The client and I find a way to acknowledge that while life is indeed "nasty, brutish, and short," it is also funny: twinkle-in-the-eye funny, sly-grin funny, laugh-till-we-cry funny...I want the connections between myself and my clients to include silence, compassion, anger, uncertainty, all that we evoke in one another. Not excluding laughter, and not limited to laughter. (p. 55)

Kubie is quite right that the sharing of humor automatically creates a powerful emotional involvement between client and therapist, but it need not be a secret one nor a damaging one. It can be a means of helping to establish a friendly, collaborative atmosphere between client and therapist, a sense of solidarity, a feeling of "He/she understands me; we are working together on this." Greenwald (1975) would add, "Your humor must be based on your liking people and your appreciation of them" (pp. 115-116).

E. Mark Stern (Ansell et al., 1981) recounted in a discussion with Mindess how he discovered that he was a funny man.

> **EMS:** I always thought of myself as a serious therapist until a session I had with a group a few years back. Just as I walked in one evening, I heard the group members joking among themselves. A man I always regarded as somewhat guarded was remarking to a depressed woman, "And is that when he nodded out on you? Oh, he nods out on me every time I talk about getting a new job." And then they started laughing. Somewhere along the line I had become not only a very funny person but an endearing one as well. I hadn't seen myself as particularly funny, but now I consider my gait—how I sit—the way I sip my tea. Hell, I'd even be funny to me.

> **HM:** When they started to perceive you as funny, did that make them more comfortable with you?

> **EMS:** I think so. I don't believe anyone lost face. It may have even encouraged an atmosphere of equality [Cf. Dreikurs, 1971; Mosak, 1984]. At any rate, it added yeast to the warm feeling my clients had toward me.

> **HM:** I would welcome my clients joking about me. But I'll bet you there are therapists who would think it was demeaning. (p. 20)

ROLE OF HUMOR IN DIAGNOSIS

> *Men show their character in nothing more clearly than in what they think laughable.*
>
> —Goethe, *Maxims*

Since all behavior occurs within the framework of the individual's life style and generally reflects it, one use of humor in therapy is in diagnosing the individual's basic convictions and characteristic way of moving through life. Adler (1927b) endorsed the comment of "that far-seeing psychologist, Dostoyevsky, [who] said that 'One can recognize a person's character much better by his laughter than by a boring psychological examination'" (p. 199). Exemplifying how a person's laughter can be a reflection of his/her life style, Adler (1927b) contrasted those who use laughter to make connections with others, with those who embitter every situation they enter. The latter "walk around as though they wish to extinguish every light" or "go through life as though they were bent by the weight of a great load" (p. 199). Always alert to the polarities of "usefulness" and "uselessness" inherent in any behavior, Adler also reminded us that even laughter and cheerfulness can be employed on the "useless" side to support an individual's defensive denial of reality or in aggressive support of his/her private fiction of superiority.

Lenzberg (1937), too, pointed out that "The nature of an individual's laughter and that which occasions it is a rich potential source of information regarding him which should not be neglected by the therapist. Laughter can be a profound 'confession' on the part of the one doing the laughing" (pp. 81-82). Some of these unknowing "confessions" can be illustrated by exploring the question of who enjoys jokes. One purpose in keeping distant from others is to show that you are special in some way, different from other people (Adler, 1963; Ansbacher & Ansbacher, 1956), as in the message conveyed by the "individualist" who proudly proclaims: "I always laugh in the movies when no one else does; the things I think are funny, no one else laughs at but me."

Some life styles (Mosak, 1972) will not permit laughter at all, e.g., people who believe that "to live is to suffer," "life is a vale of tears," and "suffering builds character." These people manage to surround themselves with unmitigated misery, either physical or emotional, and often both. But not only do the "sufferers" not laugh, but also do the moralists for whom "Life is real, life is earnest, and how can I laugh when kids are starving in Biafra?" They implicitly sit in judgment of others and thereby feel noble, demonstrating that they are more sensitive and have higher ideals than the ordinary, callous, unfeeling mortals who can still laugh "at a time like this."

A variant on the "superior moral standards" life style is the "pure as the driven snow" person, usually a woman, who either displays blushing behavior or righteous indignation at the telling of an erotically-tinged or "dirty" joke or who innocently declares "I don't get it."

Still another group of non-laughers are those for whom feelings are dangerous; they believe that one must neither laugh nor cry. To these individuals, called "controllers" by Mosak (1972, 1973) and others, feelings are lions in a cage, ready to spring loose out of control should the door be nudged open ever so slightly, even in laughter. In a study somewhat flawed by the small number of subjects, Rosenheim and Golan (1986) concluded that "obsessives stand out in the consistent, decisive repudiation of humorous interventions...Most of the hysterical and depressive patients were 'neutral'...and a minority of both groups...took a negative stand" (p. 121). Obsessives are, of course, controllers (Mosak, 1968).

In sharp contrast are the life styles where everything is funny; some of these people are the excitement seekers. They can and do transform the simplest event into the comedy scene of the year and enliven their own and other lives in this way. Among the constant laughers, too, some neurotic or psychotic individuals come to use laughter chronically as a substitute for the expression of genuine feelings and thoughts (Zuk, 1966).

Incidentally, among those who never understand jokes are those who like to be the center of attention. With everyone in the room laughing, the one who "doesn't get it" can invariably draw the attention of the group away from the joke-teller and onto himself/herself, thereby achieving the one-up position (Potter, 1951). These people may take pride in and draw attention to their *lack* of a sense of humor. Interestingly, either approach to humor—displaying it or dramatizing the lack of it—is a highly effective way to distinguish oneself from others. Levine and Rakusin (1959) found that those who are most responsive in their sense of humor are known by more of their peers, but also that unresponsiveness to humorous stimuli is an efficacious way to rescue oneself from anonymity. In both cases, the individuals are expressing the same desire to be recognized, to be "special," but one does it in such a way that the social interest is enhanced, while the other achieves recognition on the "useless" side of life.

In the category of people who do not get jokes, but without aggressive intent, are those who cannot handle two trends simultaneously, that is, those who have a "one track mind" and cannot switch tracks, some of whom are neurologically involved (Redlich et al., 1951; Roberts & Johnson, 1957) and others who merely have little or no tolerance for ambiguity. Also a joke is sometimes "too close" to be funny to him/her

(See later) (Kubie, 1971; Levine & Abelson, 1959; Levine & Redlich, 1960).

Moody (1978) described another group of "laughter-resistant individuals" who take remarks made in jest seriously. They feel that "Many a truth is often spoken in jest" and invite from the teller a disclaimer—"I was only kidding." A similar group takes the joke literally. When co-therapists tell Joke 116, most patients laugh. Some become angry and charge, "Now you're calling me a dog!"

Although not necessarily so, oftentimes an aggressive component is in the failure to understand a joke. Other hostile acts against joke-tellers include outright rejection ("Not *that* one again" or "That's not the way it goes" or "I know a *really* funny one!") and comments such as "I don't see anything funny about that," with its implication of one's own higher standards in such remarks as "You'll have to do better than that if you want to make *me* laugh." The listener is exercising his/her power of putting the joke-teller down and asserting his/her superiority. All of these forms of rejection by the nonlaugher are dysjunctive, of course, and increase the distance between people (Adler, 1927b). In a less intuitive vein, empirical studies have indicated that lack of joking ability may be useful as an indicator of stress (Smith & White, 1965) and that disturbances in humor behavior are associated with disturbances in other emotional areas (Redlich et al., 1951). O'Connell (1975) cited his research indicating that "In general, low-humor response is related to repressive life styles" (p. 185).

Asimov (1971) offered still another illustration of why some people are laughter-resistant or have no sense of humor.

> My father, on the other hand, though he had many virtues, was precisely the wrong kind of father for a budding jokester. The sad truth is that he had no sense of humor.

> There are a variety of reasons why a person might lack a sense of humor. He might be hopelessly short of intelligence or imagination and be unable to catch the sudden alteration of point of view, or fail to appreciate it if he did. My father certainly didn't fall into those classifications.

> With him, rather, it was a matter of dignity. There are some people who, for whatever reason, equate laughter with folly. They see the joke but school themselves not to laugh, and in the end they come to see no reason to laugh at all.

> And that was my father. He was dignified and, but for the fact that he was clean-shaven, had the bearing of an Old Testament patriarch. Laugh? At foolishness? Never! (p. 132)

The joke-teller's motives are not always noble nor are the results always socially conjunctive. As Wolfe (1932) noted, "humour may be diverted from its common-sense purpose of lightening the burden of existence, and become an instrument of cruelty and social disintegration...There are some people who bolster their egos with an extensive repertoire of stories told at the expense and humiliation of someone else" (pp. 185-186). Among these are ethnic jokes and racial slurs, the "dirty jokes" which often derogate women[10] as well as the more personally-tailored jabs to the heart designed to support the spurious sense of superiority of the joke-teller. Rom (1971) pointed out that some who enjoy telling jokes have no sense of humor.[11] Some controllers (Mosak, 1972, 1973) who demand center stage are accustomed to buttonholing all comers and telling them jokes at great length (they prefer multi-stage, interminable ones) to control the situation and keep attention upon themselves.

Jokes also have pragmatic uses. John F. Kennedy used one-liners effectively to avoid confrontations at press conferences, and the client may attempt to use them in much the same manner during therapy sessions.

Sharing laughter, on the other hand, is generally social conjunctive; it tends to bridge the gap between people, helps us experience the other's frame of reference, and serves an extremely valuable function in maintaining and increasing social cohesiveness. Parenthetically, it has been suggested that the Jew's ability to laugh at himself/herself and the world has contributed in no small measure to Jewish survival (Rovit, 1967). The adaptive potential of laughter as a survival mechanism and as an alternative to hostility and aggression is considerable. Perhaps we should consider subsidizing a corps of comedians to spread around the globe as

---

[10]Quantitatively, too, women are most often the butt of jokes, even in the tests of humor appreciation devised by male social scientists, according to O'Connell (Kass, 1967). He found that when he changed the tests to make men the butt of the same jokes, the men didn't think the jokes were so funny anymore. With increasing equality between the sexes (Dreikurs, 1971; Mosak & Schneider, 1977), men may become the butt of jokes, even "dirty" ones, more frequently.

[11]The writer here is reminded of a British psychiatrist who, at an international conference, announced that he was going to tell some jokes, pulled out a sheaf of papers, and *read* from them, "The first joke I'd like to tell..."

a possible antidote to war and riots, in place of the CIA![12] (Cf. Lathrop, 1981). In this country, think what a few more Bill Cosbys, Dick Gregorys, Danny Kayes, Bob Hopes, and Rodney Dangerfields could do to heal the breaches between Black and White, Gentile and Jew. One author suggested that the progress of a society might be measured by the stock jokes it no longer finds amusing (Stylites, 1950). In any case, if *homo sapiens* manage to survive the irrational and aggressive choice of our political leadership long enough to continue the evolving process, we strongly suspect that our sense of humor and ability to laugh will help us to do so.

On an individual level, people who enjoy jokes are likely to be those who have social interest (Goodchilds & Smith, 1964; Smith & White, 1965; Worthen & O'Connell, 1969), who are willing to cooperate with the joke-teller to decrease social distance. As Rom (1971) summarized the situation, "Healthy personalities will develop and use their potential humor as a friendly attitude towards forming a bond with their neighbor; neurotics and other misfits usually fail to do this and abuse humour in one form or another" (p. 229). Rosen (1963), in fact, advised that "The obsessional individual seems to have to learn to insult and be insulted gracefully before his social development can proceed" (p. 723).

The masking function of laughter and smiling has often been observed and commented upon. But Pirandello (1965) saw the humorist as the iconoclast, smasher of deceptive images, *unmasker,* exposer of the incongruities in man, and Hahn (1972) has described the reputation for wit and humor which often accompanies judicious dropping of usual images or masks.

Clinicians have frequently commented upon the defensive functions of laughter and smiling in therapy. The client may smile as a consequence of his/her private logic (Nikelly, 1971), confirmation of his/her private goal of superiority (Adler, 1958), or from suspicion. Even defensive laughter, however, because of its nature as a social imperative, can serve as a facilitator of communication—laughter invites others to be in on the joke. Rom (1971) wrote that "without intending to produce or to consume humour, a psychotherapist may often smile to himself when understanding the mental process of people around him—or of himself"

---

[12]Perhaps this suggestion is simplistic but Danny Kaye has created much good will for the United States with his performances for UNESCO in many foreign countries.

(p. 228). And so may the client. Whether the therapist or client is the one who laughs or smiles unexpectedly, such a response invites investigation from the other and can lead to fruitful dialogue between the two (Seagull, 1966; Zuk, 1964, 1966).

In informal diagnostic procedures, joking in the therapeutic hour has been used as a projective technique akin to that of the analysis of dreams or early recollections. Grossman (1970, 1977), Grotjahn (1949), and Zwerling (1955) have used the favorite joke technique in psychotherapy. Wolfe (1932) suggested that

> If you wish to test the dynamic patterns of your neighbor—it is wise to try this out on yourself first—ask for his three favorite stories, interpret the 'dynamic drift' in much the same way that you would interpret a dream, and you will learn his goal and his technique of life very quickly. (p. 187)

The technique of asking favorite jokes is also used effectively in children's psychotherapy (Orfandis, 1972; Yorukoglu, 1974).

Since in diagnosis to tap the person's assets is as important as is his/her liabilities or difficulties, humor is useful here too. Humor has been shown to be positively correlated with intelligence, insight, creativity (Dworkin & Efran, 1967; Ferris, 1972; Getzels & Jackson, 1962; Singer & Berkowitz, 1972; Smith & White, 1965), empathy, and reality contact (Roberts & Johnson, 1957), as well as general adjustment, maturity, internal locus of control, and lack of defensiveness (Lefcourt et al., 1974; O'Connell, 1960, 1964; Smith & White, 1965).

CHAPTER

ROLE OF HUMOR IN INTERPRETATION

When they're offered to the world in merry guise,
Unpleasant truths are swallowed with a will—
For he who'd make his fellow, fellow creatures wise
Should always gild the philosophic pill!

—William S. Gilbert, *Yeoman of the Guard*

Adlerians certainly agree with Gardner (1971) who cited the above message, that in an atmosphere of lightness learning is facilitated. Adler (Ansbacher & Ansbacher, 1956) said, "We have always been inclined to use jokes to clarify his error to the neurotic. In this way we can show him that he has a second frame of reference within which he acts, and that he tries to bring his problem in line with logic in accordance with this false system" (p. 252). Adler sometimes used the "Yes, but..." metaphor[13] to

---

[13]Berne (1964) has incorporated this metaphor into his game of "Why Don't You—Yes But."

describe these two frames of reference of the neurotic. The neurotic's "Yes" acknowledges that he/she knows the common sense ways of looking at life's problems and going about the solution of them, while the "but" introduces his private logic of *why* he should be excused for not doing so (Cf. Ansbacher, 1965).

Adler (1964b) also used the joke to let the client know that "he can take his trouble more lightly than he is doing" (p. 296). The Adlerian view can be contrasted with that of Kubie (1971) who warns that "Of special importance is the fact that many patients frequently use humor as a defense against accepting the importance of their own symptoms in their efforts to evade the acceptance of help" (p. 862). In our view, many clients' central problem is exactly that—not only do they "accept the importance of their own symptoms," but they *play up* the importance of their suffering and *maintain* their symptoms in order to avoid meeting the ordinary tasks of life (Shulman & Mosak, 1967). I have labeled this behavior—common in those whose hidden goal is to be First but do not believe that they can attain that position except via the moral superiority of suffering—"the substitution of 'nobility' for 'no ability.'" Humor can help such individuals take themselves and their symptoms less seriously when they need to do so.

Some jokes are useful in very specific therapeutic situations such as when dealing with the person who considers himself/herself a "born loser" or "shlemazel" (Rosten, 1968). The therapist, at an appropriate moment, might tell the story of...

> ...the man to whom everything adverse always happened, and he decided he just could not stand it any longer, so he was going to kill himself. He drove his car up to a mountain, parked it in front of a precipice, and decided to throw himself over the cliff. But before doing this terrible thing, he would make his peace with his Maker. He got down on his knees and raised his eyes to the heavens, and prayed, "Dear God, forgive me for what I am about to do, but I just can't stand it any longer. I have taken as much as I can take." Just then some birds flying overhead let go their droppings, which fell right on his head. He looked up and scolded, "You see what I mean, God?...For other people they sing!"

This kind of dramatization in the joke sometimes concretizes something for the client when a more direct statement of a verbal interpretation would fail to do so. In Rosen's (1963) words, "if a patient can first be induced to laugh, the grasping of an interpretation may become possible" (p. 715).

In addition, jokes permit us to use a mode of interpretation which may be less threatening to the client than the conventional interpretation. We can point out the source of some of his/her difficulties without making a direct interpretation which might hurt. As an example, for those whose life styles fit the pattern, Danny Thomas' jack story may be useful in helping them to see how they bring about confirmation of their own pessimistic expectations (and their number is legion or the joke would not have attained the status of "classic"). As we recall it, it went something like this:

> *A young fellow has gotten a new car, and he has a date out in the country with his girlfriend. He gets himself dressed in his new suit, gets in the car, drives, and is 8 or 10 miles out of town when suddenly his new car has a flat tire. He gets out of the car, and he's upset because his girlfriend is waiting for him, he's looking forward to showing off his new car, there's no telephone around, and he doesn't want to get his new suit dirty, but what can you do? So he opens up the trunk and lo and behold, the people who sold him the car forgot to put the jack in the trunk. Now he's very upset. What kind of a world is this? They sell you a car and don't even give you a jack anymore. Well, what can you do, his girlfriend is waiting, it is probably 8 or 10 miles back to the nearest gas station, so he starts walking down the road toward the gas station, and it begins to rain. He's even more angry, he's going to get drenched, and when he changes the tire he'll get all dirty, and his girlfriend doesn't know where he is, etc. But what can you do? So he walks a little farther, and he says to himself, "I'll go to the nearest station. I'll ask for a jack. I'll tell them my car broke down," and suddenly he has an uneasy thought: Knowing he doesn't have a jack and knowing he's stuck miles from nowhere, what if they decide they won't lend him a jack? "Well, the worst they can do is ask me for a deposit. How much is a deposit? $5? Well what the hell, I'll get it back afterwards." "But what if they ask me for $10, or $15, more money than I have? Boy, that would really be terrible. They really couldn't do that." He walks on, and then he has another thought. "Maybe they won't even give me the jack with a deposit, knowing I'm stuck out here. Maybe they'll insist on*

renting me a jack. Well, how much will it cost? A couple dollars? No, wait a minute...." Knowing he's stuck out there, maybe they'll really get him, really nail him. As he walks further, he gets even wetter, he thinks to himself, "Boy, they really got me, here I am 8 miles out of town, I got a flat tire, my girl is waiting for me, she doesn't know whether I'm living or dead...but wait a minute, maybe they won't even rent me a jack, maybe they'll say 'We'll sell you one.' If they say they'll sell me one, what can I do, I guess I'm going to have to buy one...damn automobile agency...How much can they charge me? Can't cost more than $10. But what if they decided...after all, they've got me where they want me, they can charge me anything."

After a good bit of walking and a good bit of getting wet, he finally gets to the gas station, walks in, and the gas station attendant walks up to him and says, "Yes?"

And he exclaims, "You can take your jack and shove it!"

We also may use jokes to generate enough anxiety to get things moving again or to confront a client with his/her hidden manipulations. In marital counseling, for example, where one partner clearly but overtly wants out and is "getting counseling" in order to stall for time, he/she frequently will claim concern for the partner's distress as a rationalization for avoiding the "shock" that open announcement of the desired divorce will bring. In such a situation a colleague tells the story of

...the kindly and sympathetic man with a young bulldog pup who needed to have his tail cropped. This considerate man was just too tenderhearted to chop off the dog's 12 inch tail...so he took it off one inch at a time.

A client who is overcritical and cynical about everything might be told the story of the cynic at the circus (Joke 37); a self-absorbed compulsive talker may gain insight from being told Joke 46 at an appropriate moment in his/her therapy; and the "pleaser" (Mosak, 1972) may profit from Joke 39. An adolescent or young adult locked in combat with a parent might be told the following dialogue, and be thereby assisted to move beyond that strategy for dealing with parental problems:

Father: "Going out?"

Son: "Yeah."

Father: "Have a good time!"

Son: "Why must you always be telling me what to do?"

Joke 134 may be similarly presented.

Incidentally, many of these jokes have been around long enough to remind us that jokes which rely entirely on novelty for their humorous effect are good for only one round. After the first telling, the joke is no longer funny, a factor which makes rereading an old joke book a particularly unrewarding enterprise. The joke's revitalization in the appropriate therapeutic context is not due to the surprise ending, but rather to the surprise of the patient upon finding it a relevant analogy to his/her own behavior.

Jokes in which humor lies in their relevance of our common humanity have more staying power than jokes which rely solely upon surprise to amuse us, and are more likely to be useful in the therapeutic setting. We laugh repeatedly at jokes which deal with the more universal themes of our common human experiences, feelings, and frailties, and most especially when they are salient to our own lives. Take, for example, the famous remark—a witticism calculated to appeal to the residual inferiority and superiority feelings in all of us—of Groucho Marx, who, when invited to join a country club, sent back his regrets, declining with "I wouldn't belong to a club that would have *me* for a member." Or the story of Jack Benny, known for his "miserliness." In this classic radio bit, he walks out on the street in Beverly Hills and a holdup man shoves a gun in his ribs and demands, "Your money or your life!" There's a dead silence, and the rattled holdup man demands again, "YOUR MONEY OR YOUR LIFE!" And Jack Benny unhurriedly replies, "Don't rush me. I'm thinking, I'm thinking!" The universality of the appeal lies in the fact that each of us has been confronted by troublesome situations where the only alternatives seemed to be choices we would rather not make—"between the devil and the deep blue sea," "between a rock and a hard place," "damned if I do and damned if I don't" are folk sayings expressing this kind of double bind. We can all identify with that universal feeling, laugh at ourselves, and feel closer to our brothers/sisters through the medium of the joke.

Another benefit of telling a joke to make an interpretation then, is this universalization, this transfer of individual suffering to the realm of collective suffering (Lenzberg, 1937). We become aware that this human frailty, weakness, or difficulty of ours need not be taken as seriously as we sometimes do, because other people are in the same boat we are, and our weakness is their weakness. Because the transition to such an enlarged perspective presumably signals personal growth, Shaw (1960) holds laughter to be a paradigm of personal growth.

In addition, joke-telling and other humorous interpretations often facilitate the acquisition of insight, what Mosak (1984) called the "aha experience." We have already made note of Adler's comparison of neurosis to a bad joke. Kuhlman (1984) echoes Adler's two track hypothesis and applies humor to get patients back on the right track.

> Effective therapeutic humor is like a parallel sidetrack to the main route of therapy. It takes the client off the track briefly but does not lose sight of the ongoing themes and allows easy access back to them. While on the sidetrack the client is given a slightly altered view of what is ahead *and* behind...Humor may also sidetrack the client into an entirely new direction and cause the client to lose sight of or access to the original path. The client is subjected to such a radical change of scenery that he/she becomes disoriented and cannot integrate it with what has taken place before. (p. 85)

Mindess (Ansell et al., 1981) saw humor as not only facilitating insight but also facilitating catharsis, self-acceptance, and openness in psychotherapy. Kuhlman (1984) added that humorous interpretations can be insight-facilitating because they invite the client to be an active participant in the interpretation process, an activity Adlerians encourage (Mosak, 1984), and that can sometimes bypass client resistance to change.

Weiner (1975) distinguishes between *insight strategies* and *detachment strategies,* the former encouraging patients to look more closely at their problems, the latter encouraging patients to distance themselves from them. Humor can be utilized with either strategy. Humor also can be beneficial in overcoming therapeutic resistance to change. Some patients want to prolong therapy on the basis that one can't change old behaviors ("You can't change human nature," "A leopard can't change its spots," and "You can't teach an old dog new tricks") and ideas in a short period of time. We may tell them the following story:

> *A millionaire from Long Island decides to take a motor trip to Los Angeles. He and his chauffeur drive until they arrive at the outskirts of Chicago. At this point the millionaire tells his driver, "I've changed my mind. Turn left here. I'd like to go to New Orleans instead." And you know what the chauffeur did?*

He turned around peevishly and, with a snap of the fingers, pro-
tested, "You expect me to change directions just like that?"

Another colleague plays "the crazy therapist" (O'Connell, 1975).
Told by his patient that she must not relinquish her beliefs "because God
would not want me to," he looks up to Heaven and inquires, "God is
that what you really want her to do or is it possible that...?" The
humorous approach makes the therapist's inquiry palatable, and they
then proceed to examine why the patient resists change. Still another example of "the crazy therapist" tactic appeared in Greenwald's book
(1967) in which he described how he interviewed a patient while he sat
under his desk. A colleague once made a humorous but "outrageous"
suggestion to a patient who countered laughingly, "You need a good
psychiatrist." To which the therapist replied, "You're right! Do you
know a good one?"

A French Adlerian, Herbert Schaffer (Manaster et al., 1977)
remembered, "Adler used to say to paranoid patients who believed
everyone was watching them and paying no attention to anyone else,
'Lucky you! When I go out in the street not even a dog pays attention to
me'" (p. 93).

Occasionally the patient provides the humor as we have already seen
in Stern's illustration (Ansell et al., 1981). It may take the form of a
spontaneous *bon mot,* an ironic statement of recognition or insight, or a
joke. Sometimes the laughter results from the patient's tripping up of
self.

> *A patient spends most of her waking hours staring at and*
> *meditating over a butcher knife which she places on the kitchen*
> *table every day. She ponders suicide. The therapist suggests that*
> *there are more useful ways of leading her life.*
>
> *This suggestion angers the patient who challenges, "Yeah?*
> *Like what?"*
>
> *The therapist responds, "What are your friends doing this*
> *weekend?"*
>
> *She replies that they are going to Colorado on a ski trip.*
>
> *When the therapist suggests that she could accompany*
> *them, she counters with "Yeah! And get killed on the slopes?"*

Sadie Dreikurs (Manaster et al., 1977) told a delightful story

> ...of one time when Adler interviewed the parents of a 9-year old boy. Father: "Our son is a wonderful boy—he is obedient, neat, orderly, and a wonderful student, he has many friends and he is loved by all of his family and friends." Adler: "What is his problem?" Father: "He steals." Adler then called the boy and the interview follows. Adler: "What do you steal?" Boy: "Money." Adler: "What do you do with the money?" Boy: "I buy copy books, crayons, pencils, and things like that." Adler: "But I understand that your parents buy all of these things for you." Boy: "Yes, they do, but I want to buy things with my *own money.*" (pp. 62-63)

Another example is of the patient in psychoanalytic therapy who laments, "I used to enjoy a cup of coffee in the morning but now I can't because I don't know what need I'm satisfying." An advantage of appreciation of patient humor is that "The therapist who shares in and appreciates a client's humor also validates for the client a sense of mastery and respite from pain" (Kuhlman, 1984, p. 60).

Slips of the tongue are another form of generating patient humor. And then there are the "Spoonerisms."[14] A high school freshman, discussing her English class, informs that they are studying Dickens' "Sale of Two Titties." Mosak and Gushurst (1971) have provided additional examples of how what a patient says and what a patient means might differ. Still another situation for the production of humor occurs when both therapist and client simultaneously utter the identical statement in almost echolalic fashion. Patients also express the laughter of understanding, e.g., "What kind of procrastinator am I? I'm the person they ought to send to fetch the Angel of Death. Everyone would live forever."

Freud (1960) acknowledged that the laughter of the patient sometimes signified the gaining of insight, although he assumed that the laughter was the freeing of psychic energy previously used for repression. The Adlerian would suggest that laughter results from the cognitive connection made, where previously there was none; also, perhaps from the shared understanding between therapist and client, and the pleasure and

---

[14]According to *The Random House Dictionary of the English Language,* a "spoonerism" [is] the transposition of initial or other sounds of words, usually by accident, as in *our queer old dean* for *our dear old queen* [after W.A. *Spooner* (1844-1930), English clergyman known for such slips;....]

relief from being understood and at being able to drop pretenses and accept oneself "as is." This phenomenon of a sudden, almost involuntary, smile or laugh, called by Dreikurs (1964) the "recognition reflex," is often demonstrated in the course of Adlerian family counseling sessions when the therapist discovers and discloses the purpose of a child's misbehavior (Dreikurs, Corsini, Lowe, & Sonstegard, 1959) as well as in individual psychotherapy.

TURNING THE CLIENT AROUND WITH HUMOR

"Laughter and tears are meant to turn the wheels of the same machine of sensibility; one is wind power, and the other is water power that is all."

—Oliver Wendell Holmes,
Autocrat at the Breakfast Table, 1858

Anxiety is a dysjunctive emotion which increases the distance between the individual and other people, between the individual and the tasks of life. Anxiety or fearfulness is inhibiting; it moves us back, prevents us from accomplishing whatever is required in the solution of a life task. Among the peculiarities of anxiety, according to Harry Stack Sullivan is the fact that it is always "at 180°" to any other tension with which it coincides. Thus, laughter, even "nervous laughter," may be an individual's attempt to reduce anxiety. Once a situation which has us upset and considerably worried is over, we laugh, and this turns us away from our concerns and our inability to function.[15] Hence, laughter serves to change a minus situation into a plus, to change dysjunctive feelings into conjunctive ones, to move us toward appropriate action again. Similarly in the "friendship therapy" that people do with one another, laughter also is used to try to reverse the insidious processes of anxiety and depression. The person who is worried or upset may be invited out "for a few laughs" in order to turn him/her away from own concerns. And research has empirically demonstrated the effectiveness of laughter in mitigating anxiety (Hauck & Thomas, 1972).

Tears are "water power," as both Holmes and Adler (1958) have remarked, and laughter is "wind power." We have earlier discussed the sense of power which may accrue for the joke-teller , whether he/she invokes laughter on the useless side of life by putting others down or on the useful side by drawing people closer together, while enjoying the attention drawn to himself/herself. For the therapist too, a sense of power comes from getting someone to laugh, especially someone who does not laugh easily, like the depressive.

> *"For all your ills*
> *I give you laughter."*
>
> —Rabelais

We recall in this connection the fairy tale of "The Princess Who Would Not Laugh," who controlled everyone around her with her tears and defeated a parade of suitor-princes who were determined to win her hand and half the kingdom by making her laugh. Like the princes, the therapist must exert all his/her powers to turn the depressive towards life. Robert Burton (1621/1932), in his famous classic, *Anatomy of Melancholy,* offered mirth and laughter as a cure for depression. The techniques of paradoxical intention (Buckham, 1946; Frankl, 1969) or anti-suggestion (Wexberg, 1929) may help in such a situation. In this

---

[15]An interesting point to note is that while Wolpe's (1958) theory of reciprocal inhibition is very similar to Adler's view concerning dysjunctive and conjunctive emotions, he does not include humor or laughter among the responses that might have an inhibitory effect upon anxiety.

connection Lathrop (1981) pointed out that "Humor is based upon the juxtaposition of paradoxical (opposite) images. The use of paradox in therapy is well documented" (p. 7). At an appropriate moment I sometimes tell the depressed patient a story and he/she will burst out laughing. I tease him/her—I tell the person not to laugh. He/she responds with surprise. "Why? This is the first time I've felt like laughing in a long, long time." "But if you laugh, it will spoil your depression. You know that laughter is incompatible with depression" (Cf. Hassett & Schwartz, 1977). His/her response? To laugh again. He/she will generally make some kind of joshing remark or defend himself/herself a little by saying, "Don't worry. I'll be depressed again tomorrow." And the therapist may even make light of that with something like, "That's OK, as long as you come in laughing." Laughter, more laughter, reinforcement, a circular process, and the patient begins to swing away from depression. This is an example of power on the useful side of life; the client feels good, the therapist feels good, and the therapeutic task is made easier. Frankl (1969) emphasized the role of humor in paradoxical intention, commenting, "In fact, paradoxical intention should always be formulated in as humorous a manner as possible" (p. 108). This encourages the patient to adopt "a humorous attitude toward a symptom" (p. 108). Moody (1978) speculated that "for at least a moment, a person who laughs can forget his troubles. Perhaps humor sometimes works just by withdrawing attention from pain" (p. 112). In this connection Nietszche explained, "Man alone suffers so excruciatingly in the world that he was compelled to invent laughter."

Wolfe (1932) used the joke as a task-setting technique (Mosak, 1984) to help the schizoid patient break out of the isolation of what Adler (1927a; Ansbacher & Ansbacher, 1956) called the "witches' circle." To get the client to practice involvement with other people, Wolfe prescribed the following:

> Find a good story and tell it to at least one person during the day. If the first person you tell the story to does not laugh, continue until you have made someone laugh. If you cannot find anyone to laugh at your stories there is a danger that your sense of humor is perverted. Get someone to tell you a story that he thinks is amusing. Tell this story to someone else until you have established the communal bond of good humor. Continue this prescription until you have experienced the reward of citizenship in the republic of laughter. (pp. 187-188)

Not all humor in therapy is in the form of jokes—not even the major part of it, in fact. The best of therapeutic humor is more personally tailored to the individual and his/her situation in and out of therapy, to the state of the therapist-patient relationship at the moment, and at the same time retains the universal quality represented by jokes at their best.

A major difficulty of many male clients, for example, is in the realm of concern for their masculinity. Adler (1958), who coined the term "masculine protest," pointed out that the inequality of the sexes in this society not only has deleterious effects on the female who feels keenly her inferior status, but upon the male who becomes preoccupied with establishing his sexual superiority (Mosak & Schneider, 1977). One form which male sexual difficulty takes is called the "Don Juan complex." Adler described other expressions of the masculine protest in both men and women in his *Problems of Neurosis* (1964a) as do other Adlerians. Rycroft (1969) cited the joke "Any man that can't find what he's looking for in a thousand women is really looking for a boy," which alludes to the analytic suspicion of, and search for, "latent homosexuality." The Adlerian version, since Adlerians do not subscribe to the concept of "latent" homosexuality (Cf. Mosak, 1983), is that "Two women are fewer than one." That is, when a man cannot make up his mind between two or more women, he wishes to escape the responsibility of the marriage task.

For the male who is more openly overconcerned about his manhood, I have devised a humorous way of dealing with the problem and bringing about a change in perspective. I tell him of the Mosak Instant Sure-Fire Test of *Real* Masculinity. Its instructions state that the patient is to "go home, stand in front of a full length mirror, and drop your pants." The criterion measure is "If there's something hanging between your legs, you pass!" From that humorous beginning, we explore and the patient is helped to discard his outmoded and destructive ideas of what "a *real* man must do or be in his relations with others to be '*truly* masculine.'" The therapist may refer to the exaggerations of others with similar problems, e.g., the case of the man who revealed that he felt sexually inadequate because "when I make love to a woman, I want her to faint," to show the individual that he shares the same difficulty with other human beings. When the therapist and client laugh together about the mistaken notions that people hold, the therapist is implicitly conveying the message that you and I have the same problems in some degree and that one's own mistaken notions are often *exaggerations* of personality ideals which can be laughed at and corrected.

O'Connell (1972) has pointed out that exaggeration is a necessary technique of wit and humor, and suggests, analogously, "It may be that the practice of overstating and understanding a patient's views in an atmosphere of mutual respect and equality is the hallmark of the outstanding therapist. Mimicking the patient (Ansell et al., 1981) and other forms of exaggeration (Mosak & Shulman, 1974), while requiring therapists to walk tightropes lest they harm a patient, are often used effectively by many therapists.

One such light-hearted way of exaggerating and thereby dramatizing central elements in a life style is Mosak's (1984) technique of awarding "gifts" to individual clients or members of his groups at appropriate times, e.g., a Confederate flag to "the rebel of the month," a tin cup to the perpetual "beggar" for the group's attention or aid, an Avis button proclaiming "We try harder" for second children. Lifschitz (1981) described a similar tactic which led to a breakthrough in the therapy of "an intense, very sensitive, and bright psychologist."

> I slowly reached into my shopping bag and pulled out my fake nose and glasses, and slipped them on. I then asked him to open his eyes slowly. He looked at me and instantly exploded into a deep heartfelt spontaneous laughter that filled the room. He couldn't stop laughing and soon was wiping tears that were streaming down his face...Yet something happened in that room that was utterly liberating and transforming for Dan and myself. There was spontaneity, a trusting of one's own sense of humor, a risking of being crazy, that would never be forgotten by either one of us. (p. 78)

In addition to gifts, Mosak also gave clients "names" which correspond to the essence of their life style. Overambitious drivers may be designated as "Superman;" a person who knows best because he/she is always right may be labeled as "Mr. (or Mrs.) God." A person with no challenges left but who lives only for overcoming challenges may be referred to as "St. George with no dragons to slay." The atmosphere of mutual respect (Mosak & Mosak, 1978), equality (Dreikurs, 1971), and we might add, affection (Mosak, 1984), is of course essential as a background for such tactics; the laughter must be *with* and not *at* the client. As Kubie (1971) aptly noted, no underlying hostility can exist in the therapist when he/she jests with the client or the latter will immediately cut through the pseudohumor, detect, and respond to the hostility. In addition, whether making interpretations via jests or "gifts" or "names," the therapist must have a feel for the rightness of the moment, as with any interpretation.

Another light-hearted technique described by Mosak (1984) is "creating images" for the client which symbolize the life style pattern of movement or a particular strategy that individual employs. Sometimes the image permits the person to solve a previously thorny problem. An example of one of these personalized metaphors appears in the following story told by Kadis (Manaster et al., 1977):

Another recollection is of my last encounter with Adler in 1936, in Vienna. He asked me to meet him at the Hotel Regina and tell him all about the Adlerian movement in the Baltic states. I was sorry to bring the disappointing news that things were very bad. I described the various problems and concluded by saying that we would probably have to close our doors. After a few moments, Adler, in his usual quiet way, said, "What do you do when you have urgent work somewhere and the weather is terrible? Do you stay home because of rain, hail, or a real blizzard?" Although this question puzzled me, I decided on a "straight" answer, "Certainly not. If it is important enough, I put on a heavy coat and galoshes, take a rain hat or umbrella, and go out." "Isn't this the same situation? If it is important enough, why not put on your most protective clothing and proceed?" I laughed.....(p. 94)

The metaphor can be combined with giving a person a "name." We have described one client as "playing Sherlock Holmes to your own Moriarity." The client was devoted to ferreting out his own "villainy." He was a relentless detective, always on the trail of himself. Each time the client discovered another of his past and present "crimes," the therapist made allusion to the metaphor.

Twisted adages are used in a similar way in Adlerian therapy and modified to fit a particular client. In this technique, a common folk saying is twisted to illustrate the client's private logic or to make a therapeutic point, e.g., "If at first you don't succeed, try lousing it up again." A perfectionistic person or a non-risk taker may come to see that he/she is operating on the philosophy that "Nothing ventured, nothing lost." Other such adages are:

> *The best offense is a good pretense.*
> *Believing is seeing.*
> *If I knew you were coming, I'd have faked an ache.*
> *Do unto others before they do unto you.*
> *If you can keep your head while all about you are*
>   *losing theirs, brother, you don't understand the*
>   *situation.*
> *Where there's hope, there's life.*

From there, the therapist can go on to explore with the client the dynamics of the behavior, and begin training for the "courage to be imperfect" (Lazarsfeld, 1927/1966). This approach may also be helpful with those whose pattern is to feel depressed and "guilty" over their bad behavior. Once the client is able to laugh, he/she can be helped to see the purposiveness of "feeling bad" *instead* of changing the troublesome behavior, and that he/she can choose more satisfying behaviors.

The cartoon presents another form for transmitting humor. Kadis and Winick (1973) expressed the opinion that

> The success of the cartoon in psychotherapy is not necessarily linked with any phase of treatment but rather to its presentation to a patient whose continuing verbosity is self-defeating. The cartoon may be helpful if it illuminates a core problem or an issue of life style'' (p. 108).

POT- SHOTS NO. 786.

DON'T GET WELL
TOO SOON

YOUR SUFFERING
IS AN INSPIRATION
TO US ALL.

Ashleigh
Brilliant

© BRILLIANT ENTERPRISES 1975.

They feel that this method is especially suitable for "patients who have 'been around' and had considerable therapy who are likely to be able to talk about and around their difficulties without any necessary insight and/or improvement in their life situation" (p. 108). Other forms of transmitting humor are Ashleigh Brilliant's Pot-Shot Cards[16] puppetry, and clowns[17] (Moody, 1978). Ellis (1977, 1981) introduced fun and rational-emotive songs into his therapy to make certain points.

---

[16]A starter set and catalogue are available for $2.00 from Brilliant Enterprises, 117 West Valerio Street, Santa Barbara, CA 93101

[17]Ouellet, a priest and Adlerian therapist, often dons the clown costume.

In addition to the special jokes created by the therapist especially for use with a particular client, there are other "private jokes" which develop between client and therapist in the course of therapy. Van Dusen (1961) illustrated how a particular phrase or gesture (e.g., "click-click" or making sucking noises) may come to symbolize a shared insight or meaningful interpretation and result in shared laughter. Often these private jokes relate to previous troubles now becoming alleviated or outmoded attitudes or behaviors which have recently been revised. Bonime (1962, p. 42) gave the example of a woman with mousey demeanor whose self-effacing request for "another olive" was the straw that broke a friend's patience with her and led to exposure of the client's characteristic manipulative and very demanding way of operating among other people. The phrase, "another olive," became a code-phrase for any aspect of this behavioral syndrome which came to light thereafter in the therapeutic sessions. The laughter between therapist and client over these symbols is a sharing of pleasure in the client's having been able to move toward discarding a once-fixed neurotic interaction pattern or system of beliefs.

In addition, the "In-joke" between therapist and client carries the same message as it does for any in-group, that "We're in a special relationship," thus maintaining and increasing raport.

CHAPTER 7

HUMOR AS A CRITERION FOR TERMINATION

Jokes grow best on the graves
of old anxieties.

—Martin Grotjahn, 1972

Mindess (Ansell et al., 1981) suggested that "the expression of humor may also be a sign of how far along therapy is. It may be a sign that the therapy is approaching its termination" (p. 22). Adlerians use this criterion as well as the final dream (Rosenthal, 1959), and the changes in early recollections (Mosak, 1958). From the Adlerian point of view, Olson (1976) was of the opinion that

> The establishment or return of a positive sense of humor may well be considered a goal, or at least a highly desirable by-product, of psychotherapy, and the degree to which the sense of humor becomes established may be considered one criterion of the success of therapy. (pp. 34-35)

Meerloo (1966) told of a catatonic patient who "after years of absolute silence one day burst out into a laughter that contaminated all the other patients on the floor. His laughter heralded the end of his year-long game of silent withdrawal. Indeed, three weeks later, the patient was able to be discharged." While therapeutic progress is rarely that sudden or dramatic, clinicians characteristically confirm that a clear correlation often exists between increasing mental health and the ability to laugh at oneself (Cassell, 1974; Fried, 1970; Grotjahn, 1966, 1971).

Tibullus noted 2000 years ago that "It is difficult to fashion a jest with a sad mind," and modern researchers have confirmed that emotional factors interfere with our ability even to comprehend jokes (Byrne et al, 1962; Levine & Abelson, 1959; Levine & Redlich, 1960; Smith & White, 1965). If a joke generates more anxiety than the individual feels able to cope with, the person may fail to understand the joke, may distort the point of it, or may become upset by it. Too close an identification with the subject of a joke may eliminate humor, as can be seen from the following incident recounted by a therapist.

I saw a depressed adolescent girl about 17, who just could not make any decisions about anything. In the very early stages of treatment, when I tried to interpret to her, I soon learned that that was a losing proposition, so I told her a story about indecisive people, the story of...

...the itinerant farmhand who came to a farm and asked for a job. The farmer, needing somebody, said, "Sure, I'd like you to go out with the other hands into the cornfield and pick corn," which he did. At the end of the day, this new hand had picked twice as much corn as any other farmhand, and the farmer was very pleased.

The next day he reported for work and the farmer sent him out to milk the cows. This man had a magic touch; by the end of the day he had broken the farm record for how much milk he had collected. The farmer thought it over that night and said to himself, "This man is really a jewel. I'd like to keep him. I'll give him a break tomorrow; after all, I don't want to overwork him, I'll make it easy."

The next day the farmer took him to the barn where there was a big mound of potatoes and a table with various size holes and baskets underneath, and he said, "I want you to size these potatoes—put the little

*potatoes in the little holes and the big potatoes in the big
holes, etc., because we sell these things by size.''*

*Before noon the farmhand was knocking at the
farmer's door, demanding, "I want my wages; I quit!''*

*And the farmer was surprised by this. He said,
"How come? After all, I wanted to keep you here, you
do such a nice job, so today just to show you my appreciation, I gave you an easy job.''*

*"Easy job!'' replies the farmhand, "You call that
easy, all day long making decisions?''*

She burst into tears; she couldn't see this as funny at all. Later in
treatment she mentioned this incident of several months past
and indicated that she is telling the story to her friends; they find
it very funny and she thinks it's a hilarious story now. I said to
her, "How come? Several months ago you didn't see it this way.
She gave an answer which makes sense in terms of this theory.
She said, "When you first told it to me, I only felt sympathy for
this man; I could see how he felt, he felt just like I felt.'' There
was no incongruity with her feelings—it was exactly the feeling
that she had, therefore, it was not one bit funny. Now that it is
no longer her feeling, it is incongruous with her feelings; now
that she makes decisions she can afford to laugh and she sees the
humor in it.

Asimov provided an explanation in terms of two-track theory.

Sometimes the alteration in point of view is a flicker, rather than a curve or
angle. That is, there is a moment when the punch line seems to make sense and
then suddenly does not. If it makes sense, there is no alteration in point of view
and no joke, but if it doesn't...

It is the quick flip from sense to no-sense that is itself the change in point of view
and that brings the laugh...The greater the subtlety of the sense/no-sense shift
and the greater the ease with which it is caught, the better the laugh. (p. 68)

We have to agree with Grotjahn and amend Shakespeare's "He jests at
scars, that never felt a wound'' to read "He jests most at scars who has
recovered from his wound.''

The clinicians' impression that increasing "good humor" signals approaching termination is confirmed by researchers who find the wit to be an active participator and contributor to groups, more resistant to group pressure, with a high positive self-image (Goodchilds, 1972). But then Hippocrates knew that all along. In his humoral theory he described the correlation between excesses of the humors (body fluids) and temperament. A person whose humors were in balance and therefore possessed of a good temperament would have been described by him as "good humored."

CHAPTER 8

HUMOR AND
THE THERAPIST'S SKILL

The treatment of humor in the psychotherapy literature contains an abundance of "cautions," "dangers," "risks," and "contraindications" which may be likened to those warnings observed by a cross-country hauler of nitroglycerine. And if we maintain this simile, Kubie's advice (1971) would be to almost entirely forego hauling it. Actually these cautions, while valid in many instances, are greatly exaggerated. Humor presents no more dangers nor greater dangers than hauling other cargo. We recognize that dangers exist when we interpret, whether correctly, inadequately, too late, too early, in the wrong form, or with the wrong client and, with the major exception of the Rogerians and many behaviorists, we nevertheless do not prohibit the use of interpretation. All psychotherapy is a risky enterprise for all participants and both the therapist and client must take their individual risks if therapy is to succeed. Erv Polster, Narboe (1981) has told us, was especially gifted in the realm of risk-taking humor:

> Our usefulness as therapists lies in the range between what is expected and what is intolerable. Too safe and there's no reason to move; too risky and there's no support for movement.

Erv Polster walking that line: There's the session he began by asking a conventional lady, "Did you bring your teeth?" There's the man whose boring story Erv interrupted by asking, "Did you ever fuck an animal?" The man hadn't, but he sure got livelier. There's the woman who'd worked out what to say well in advance whom he taunted with, "What's on your alleged mind?" Erv won't not be considered. He is there and you have to speak taking him into account. He uses humor to demand contact.

I used to listen to Erv with my mouth hanging open, "You can't say that!" sounding over and over in my head. He can and does. Erv trusts the client's ability to support him/herself; he trusts himself to calibrate when to provoke, when to support. And he trusts that messes can be recovered from. (p. 56)

Treatment of whatever kind and specific methods of treatment have their potential for harming, and the skillful, ethical practitioner will aim at avoiding harm. This leads to an important distinction, that between harming and hurting patients. Every medical student is exposed to Hippocrates' admonition, *"Primum non nocere!—Above all, do no harm!"* Hippocrates, however, did not proclaim, "Do no hurt!" Had he done so, many of our diagnostic and surgical procedures would today not be permissible. For the purpose of illuminating this distinction, hypnosis and psychotropic drugs may harm but not hurt. Dentistry, well-practiced, may hurt but not harm. Electroconvulsive therapy may both hurt and harm. Imagine the pleasure of going to the dentist or physician if he/she had to observe, "Above all, do no hurt!" Adherence to such a principle would probably lead to the extinction of the profession. In the interest of helping our patients, while our methods may occasionally inflict hurt, the ultimate goal of the practitioner is to help, not harm. The distinction between hurt and harm may help clarify why such therapists as Ellis (1981), Farrelly and Brandsma (1974), Polster (Narboe, 1981), and some Adlerians (Mosak & Shulman, 1974) may resort to wit which others may criticize as being harmful where the above practitioners may see it as helpful, though hurtful.

Lily Gondor (Manaster et al., 1977) described a counseling session in which Adler used paradoxical intention with a child. The girl was brought to the child guidance center because she would not swallow what she was eating. In doing so, she captured the attention of her whole family at the table.

After having interviewed the mother, he brought the child in and said to her, "This is what your mother told me, that you keep the food in the mouth, and you don't want to swallow it. Everyone is upset at the table. You know, you could do something better, get much more attention, when you spit what you have in your mouth on the table. Then everyone would be upset and wouldn't talk about anything else, but about you." This would be, in part, what we call "paradoxical therapy." But now comes the interesting part. The very same thing that I am now quoting, if said by another person, may have been sadistic, unpleasant, or critical, but with Adler it was interesting. Nobody ever had the feeling that this was done in order to hurt anybody's feelings. (p. 84)

We must agree that humor can hurt. We speak of "barbed humor," "biting wit," sarcasm, "put-down" humor, and aggressive humor. Ellis (1981) explained,

RET, however, is also hard-headed and biting, because people tend to hang on to their nutty ideas powerfully and stubbornly and it often takes some bit to dislodge these notions. So humor can be useful in hard-headedly providing a realistic, more sensible philosophy for stubbornly self-battered clients. (p. 30)

In his *Anatomy of Melancholy,* Burton (1621/1932) cautioned against these "scurrile jests," and it is incumbent upon the therapist to avoid releasing his/her own aggressions upon the client or to find his/her own superiority over the client through the medium of humor. The therapist must not be a graduate of the Joan Rivers-Don Rickles school of comedy.

Two further distinctions are made by some humor theorists. First, to laugh *with* the client is both possible and permissible, but one should not laugh *at* the client. Second, one can also laugh at the perpretrator's acts and still not laugh at the perpetrator. The first becomes transparent when patient and therapist laugh together, although even here the therapist must exercise care in assessing whether the client's laughter is genuine. Kuhlman (1984) cautioned in this regard that therapists should be aware that forced or "canned laughter" may "signal illusions of in-sight and mastery" (p. 60). The patient may laugh in order to be polite, to please or to avoid offending the therapist, or to avoid admitting that he/she doesn't understand the point the therapist is making.

When the patient feels laughed at, according to Kuhlman (1984), the reason is because the patient has misunderstood the "play signals" or because the patient is already antagonistic and refuses to accept them. As Mollie used to say under such circumstances to Fibber McGee, "T'ain't funny, McGee!" Schwartz (1981) offered a different view:

The risk that a psychotherapist's humor may be misunderstood ought to be properly balanced by my hunch that the patient is probably tuned in to the countertransference. In my practice, I've learned to get a reading on how the pa-tient receives my message. I most often find it prudent to ask the patient what she/he hears me saying. (p. 79)

The second also involves a balancing act. Ellis (1981) and others have said that they do it well; other therapists do not perceive themselves as skillful balancers. The skill required bears resemblance to St. Paul's advice—"Judge ye the sin and not the sinner"—which in psychological rendition has become "distinguish between the deed and the doer." Religious or psychological, the distinction constitutes an ideal rather than a completely feasible practice.

Both therapist and patient can hide behind humor (Moody, 1978), each denying his/her feelings. Both can cloak real feelings, using humor as a suit of armor. In this manner they can cover up hurt and pretend that the other touched or did not touch a raw nerve. Humor also may permit patients to turn the therapy interview into a joke-telling session; therapists may aid and abet them for a variety of reasons, especially if the former enjoy hearing or telling a good story so much that they lose sight of their therapeutic function. The client may relate a joke in order to test the therapist. If a therapist shows amusement, the patient may attempt to convert the interview into a joke session; if the therapist by his/her demeanor conveys, "We are not amused," the patient may perceive the therapist as aloof, cold, distant, non-appreciative or rejecting (Kuhlman, 1984).

Adlerian therapists tend to share the belief that humor in therapy can be useful in a number of ways: establishing rapport, diagnosis, interpretation, and reorienting the client toward creating a better future for himself/herself. Not all analysts are leery of humor, either (Grotjahn, 1966; Ricks, 1969; Rose, 1969; Rosen, 1963). Grotjahn (1971), for example, felt that when the therapist and the patient do not laugh together, something is missing in the therapy.

Errors are sometimes made; sometimes clients "don't get it" or don't see the analogy, or are "too close" to a joke to think it is funny. But then, errors also are made in the opposite direction by those oriented to grimness and austerity (Kubie, 1971). In fact, errors are made by *all* therapists, but clients have a remarkable ability to survive therapeutic errors, if they wish to survive them—and when they don't, they will leave therapy whether errors are committed or not. In Adlerian therapy, errors are not seen as disastrous, since the therapist is a fellowperson, not God or even "The Expert." One of Kubie's objections to the use of humor in offering interpretations is that if the interpretation is presented humorously and the client takes it seriously, this is "tantamount to correcting the therapist." Nothing is wrong with that, either; in fact, "guessing" is encouraged in Adlerian therapy, beginning in the initial session (Dailey, 1966), and the client quickly learns to correct the therapist. No better way exists for the client to learn that he/she is actively working *with* the therapist, not having the therapist work *for* or *at* or *on* him/her. At the same time, the therapist is demonstrating belief in "the courage to be imperfect" and modeling the willingness to take risks.

Even among those who agree that humor in therapy should not be suppressed, differences of opinion do occur as to whether the artful use of humor in therapy is the native gift of a rare therapist, or whether it can be trained. Joanne Greenberg (Rubin, 1972), alias Hannah Green, speaking of Frieda Fromm-Reichman, described their "one running difference of opinion on which neither of us ever gave ground":

> She held that psychiatry was a science and I said it was an art. She believed that the gifts she has—humor, empathy, indignation, intuition, a first-rate intellect, linguistic sensitivity, and the endearing quality of not exploiting her patients to prove herself or her theories—she believed that these things could be taught and learned, and that anyone who was reasonably intelligent could cultivate them to a degree equal to or exceeding her own. I think she was wrong...She liked to use her face and voice to mimic—sometimes to satirize parts of both the sick and the reasonable worlds. Her satire was balanced and never used in malice....Frieda's hallmark was an artist's—a light touch. Her genius was to bring it to her work whole and as naturally as breathing. (pp. 206-7)

We believe with Fromm-Reichman that such "gifts" can be learned (indeed, Kubie mentions the great difficulty in getting young psychiatric residents *not* to pick up such behavior and try it out when they observe it being done by experienced therapists). Some of the *elan* in Fromm-Reichman described by Greenberg, which exists in other therapists with the same "gifts," is a natural accompaniment of what Csikszentmihalyi (1975) described as a "flow experience" and Shaw (1960) called the "delight phenomenon," where behavior exceeds competence so much as to take it for granted. That is a therapist who has found himself/herself able to help people *does* enjoy the work; and the therapist's laughter, sense of humor, and delight in the therapeutic work convey a sense of ease, self-confidence, and freedom. These qualities give the client increased confidence in the helping ability of the therapist, rapport spirals upward, and the end results are more likely to be the desired therapeutic benefits. This delight phenomenon cannot be faked, however—it is dependent on what Shaw called the "manageability of contradiction," the ability to handle the discrepancy between aspirations and accomplishment—and here the "courage to be imperfect" is a necessary part of it.

Not to be overlooked, then, is the essential aspect of the therapist as model. If true, as has been often suggested, that "much of the work of psychotherapy is accomplished through the process of identification" (Shoben, 1960), then the therapist's penchant for laughing at himself, accepting his own foibles, and using humor to show his obvious enjoyment of life and of the therapeutic work rather than merely making the session amusing, entertaining, and pleasant for the therapist, as Kubie suggested, facilitates the client's growth in these directions.

Whether or not humor is a "gift" or an acquired skill, therapists who use it must be comfortable with it and take delight in it. If they don't, if they feel that they can't tell a joke, or if they never remember punchlines, then they ought to avoid the injection of humor into therapy. Such therapists may utilize other forms of accomplishing whatever humor does in therapy. Humor must be part of the therapist's natural "style." If this caution is not observed, then the therapist may encounter the following:

> *A new prisoner is taking his first meal in prison. As he is eating his dinner, he hears other prisoners shout out numbers, "28," "45," "92." As each number is called, it is met with varying degrees of laughter from the other prisoners. The new prisoner, curious, asks the prisoner next to him, "What's going on? What's all this number-calling?" The other prisoner replies, "The prison library only has one joke book in which all the jokes are numbered. Since everyone has read the joke book and everyone knows the jokes, instead of telling the joke, we just call out the number. If you like the joke, you laugh." Right after dinner the new prisoner scurried over to the library, read the joke book, and memorized the numbers of some jokes he liked. The following morning at breakfast he was prepared. The number-calling began. "39" was greeted with gales of laughter. "66" and more laughter. The new prisoner shouted, "84" and complete silence met it. "What's the matter?" he asked the prisoner next to him. "I thought 84 was a great joke. How come no one laughed?" "Well, it's like this. Some people can tell a joke and some can't."*

We have few definitive answers with respect to the use of humor in psychotherapy. Those who find delight in it will continue to use it and provide rationales for doing so; those who don't, won't, and will find rationales for not introducing it in psychotherapy. Adlerians will continue to use it, study it, and attempt to explain it. Frankl (1969), who was in the Adlerian camp prior to his concentration camp experience, although he was speaking of humor in the context of paradoxical intention, endorsed the use of humor:

Humor is indeed a definitely human phenomenon. After all, no beast is capable of laughing. What is even more important humor allows man to create perspective, to put distance between himself and whatever may confront him. By the same token, humor allows man to detach himself from himself and thereby to attain the fullest possible control over himself. (p. 108)

Part C

JOKES

USED IN

PSYCHOTHERAPY

CHAPTER 9

JOKES

The jokes listed are some of those which the author has used in teaching and in psychotherapy. Some of the jokes, in addition, have been studied in terms of the structure and content of humor. The reader will observe that in the latter category many of the stories revolve about how psychology and psychotherapy, therapists and clients are portrayed in jokes. Redlich and Bingham (1960) and Perr (1973) have displayed similar interests in their study of how psychotherapists are portrayed in jokes and cartoons.

The reader will not find all of the jokes funny because first, there are "Different Jokes for Different Folks" (Hassett & Houlihan, 1979) and, second, because they include sick jokes, ethnic, and disparagement jokes. I have decided to include these for the same reason that Asimov (1971) included such in his *Treasury of Humor,* in which he wrote,

> Here is another example which I remember because when it was told, many in the audience laughed while I felt outraged. (Why do I include jokes that outraged me? Because I am not the final authority and *you* may find it funny. And further, because a joke that isn't funny may be every bit as instructive to the would-be jokester as one that is.) (p. 50)

No particular order or categorization has been used in the following listing of jokes, since a particular story may be used by the imaginative teacher or therapist in several contexts or for several of the purposes described in the text of this book.

An additional suggestion to the reader: one way to compile your own file of jokes and add to the jokes in this book is to collect the favorite jokes of clients. Such jokes may prove especially useful with other clients who have similar problems or personality dynamics, and, in any case, will encourage the client's social interest and facilitate his/her entrance into the "republic of laughter."

Say, have you heard the one about...?

1

Psychiatry is the art of teaching people how to stand on their own feet while reclining on couches. (Shannon Fife in *The Saturday Evening Post*).

2

Psycho-ceramics is that branch of psychology which deals with crackpots.

3

A *psychiatrist* is a man you pay to ask you questions your wife would ask for nothing.

4

A *psychologist* is a man who, when a naked girl enters the room, watches everyone else's expression.

5

An *architect* is a man with an edifice complex.

6

A *meteorologist* is a man who can look at a girl and predict whether.

Psychiatric examination: A checkup from the neck up (Richard Wheeler in *Look,* January 26, 1965).

Group therapy is a place where schizophrenics come to exchange hallucinations.

Ambivalence: Watching your mother-in-law drive your brand new Cadillac over a cliff.

Dancing is a form of sublimation of sexual intercourse. It is naval (navel) engagement with no seamen (semen) lost. (This one is better said than read.)

Modesty consists of letting others find out for themselves how great you are.

Chutzpah is the quality characterized by the young man who killed his father and mother and then threw himself on the mercy of the court because, after all, he was an orphan.

Frustration is the feeling you get the first time you can't do it a second time. *Panic* is the feeling you get the second time you can't do it the first time.

A *neurotic* is a person who worries about things that didn't happen in the past instead of worrying about something that won't happen in the future, like normal people.

The neurotic builds castles in the air, the psychotic lives in them, and the psychiatrist collects the rent.

16

A *neurotic* is a person who is full of should.

17

The psychotic believes that 2 + 2 = 5. The neurotic knows that 2 + 2 = 4, but he/she hates it.

18

Not all delusions are held by psychotics. I once knew a man who was under the delusion that he was a horse, and he was a stable personality.

19

Psychosis (psychoanalytic definition): Flipping one's id.

20

Malingerer's theme song: If I'd known you were coming, I'd have faked an ache.

21

Kleptomania is a strange disease; you can't take anything for it.

22

A *hypochondriac* is a person who can't leave being well enough alone.

23

Omnipotence: There but for the grace of God, goes God.

24

The wealthy Mrs. Montgomery was giving a party and everybody who was anybody was invited. To add luster to the occasion she telephoned the world-renowned violinist, Vladimir Epshtein, and asked him how much he would charge to play at the party. His fee, he told her, was $10,000. "That's very agreeable, but I want you to know that I'm hiring you to play, not to mix with my guests." "In that case my fee is only $5,000."

25

Car Bumper Sticker: "Support mental health or I'll kill you."

26

Did you hear about the cannibal with the nervous stomach? His psychiatrist said he was fed up.

27

The optimist: "Pass the cream."

The pessimist: "Pass the milk."

The cynic: "Pass the pitcher."

28

A man had twin sons, one a pessimist and one an optimist. On Christmas morning, he took them downstairs to see what Santa had left them. The three of them came to one door, which father had opened, and there was every toy imaginable. Father thought his pessimistic son would jump for joy. Instead, he stood there with a glum expression. The father asked him why he did not appear happier. The boy replied, "They are only toys."

"But," said father, "there are so many toys there, they would delight any boy."

"Nah, they would only break anyway."

The father, fed up with his pessimistic son, took the optimistic boy to the next room opened it, and there, to his dismay, he found that the floor was covered to a depth of six inches with horse manure. The father was visibly upset and thought it was a dirty trick for Santa to play. As he looked over to his son, he noticed that his son was jumping for joy.

"What are you so happy about?" asked the father.

"Gee, with all that horse manure around, Santa must have left me a horse."

29

Patient: "I have a terrible memory. I can't remember anything from one minute to the next."

Therapist: "How long has this been going on?"

Patient: "How long has *what* been going on?"

30

There's a psychologist who is studying memory. This is his area of specialization, and he hears that there's an Indian with a remarkable memory who sells pottery at the railroad station in Albuquerque. This Indian allegedly remembers everything that ever came into the scope of his perception—anything he ever saw, anything he ever heard, anything that came within his psychological field, he remembers. The psychologist decides he'd like to confirm these reports, so on his next trip West he gets off the train in Albuquerque, and, sure enough, there is this old Indian. He walks up to him, introduces himself as a psychologist who is studying memory. He then asks the Indian, "Tell me, what did you have for breakfast two years ago yesterday?"

And the Indian says, "Two years ago yesterday I had eggs."

Just then the engine toots, and the psychologist has to run back and board the train and can't follow up this questioning. But he isn't very impressed, because you ask most people you know, "What did you have for breakfast?" and they might answer "eggs," and go prove that it isn't true. Five years later, he's traveling through the Southwest and his train happens to stop in Albuquerque again. He gets off and there's his friend the Indian standing there selling pottery. He walks up to the Indian with a big smile on his face, raises his hand in Indian salutation and says "How!"

And the Indian looks at him and says "Scrambled."

The new Indian agent walked out on the reservation and saw an Indian sleeping under a tree. Nudging him awake, the agent demanded, "Why don't you go to work?"

"Why should I go to work?"

"You'd earn some money."

"Why would I want to earn money?"

"If you earned money, you could put some away for your retirement."

"Why would I want to do that?"

"Then you could lie under a tree and sleep."

"But I'm doing *that* already!"

32

Two psychiatrists meet, shake hands, and one says, "You're fine. How am I?"

33

A 75-year-old man goes to see his doctor with the request that the doctor lower his sex drive. "You're 75 and you want your sex drive *lowered?*"

"Yes, right now it's all up here" (pointing to his head).

34

The first mate of a freighter on watch during the night crossing the wintry Atlantic fortified himself against the raw wind with a spot of rum.

The next day when the captain relieved him he discovered the bottle and demanded of the mate, "Were you drinking on duty last night?"

The mate admitted taking a nip, whereupon the captain wrote in the log, over the mate's protest, "The mate was drunk last night." The captain refused to listen to the mate's protest.

The next morning the mate relieved the captain and had his sweet revenge. He wrote in the log, "The captain was sober yesterday."

35

A woman goes to the doctor because she has some pains in her back and she is not feeling well. She leaves the living room that night and her husband goes looking for her. The door of the bathroom is open and he decides to look in there; perhaps she's in there. Sure enough, she is. She's sitting in the bathtub taking a bath, and she's counting her rosary beads. He looks at her and asks, "What's this all about?"

And she says, "Well, I can't help it; the doctor said to take a bath every day religiously."

36

An amateur hypnotist is performing before an audience. He asks half-a-dozen people to come up on the stage. He waves his heirloom watch in front of them like a pendulum and all six immediately go into a trance. Impressed by his own success, he decides that he will really give the audience a show. He walks out into the audience, swinging his watch, and in a minute or two the entire audience has gone into a trance. Deciding to continue with the next part of the demonstration, he starts up the stairs of the stage. However, he trips, and his knee comes down and smashes his watch to bits. Surveying the damage to the watch and to himself, he expostulates. "Oh shit!" You know, it's two months since, and they still haven't finished cleaning up the theater yet!

37

A cynic went to the circus with a friend. Throughout the entire performance, the cynic sat on his hands while everyone applauded. He was not impressed by any of the acts in any of the three rings. His friend tried to encourage him to find some pleasure in the performance, but he found none. He had seen everything and he had seen it done better. Finally, the ringmaster came out and said, "We are now going to have an act that has never been done before. Since the act is so dangerous, we ask everyone to remain perfectly silent so that the performer will not be distracted." There was a roll of drums, the lights in the arena were extinguished, and a spotlight pointed to the top of the arena. There was a tightrope, and on the tightrope a tightrope walker was poised to take the first step. A hush fell over the audience. The tightrope walker began to walk across the rope, keeping his balance, when suddenly midway he lost his balance and began to fall. A gasp escaped from the audience. Then, suddenly, in the midst of his fall the tightrope walker caught the rope with his teeth, reached into his shirt, pulled out a violin, and began to play. There was thunderous applause. The audience rose to its feet—with the exception of the cynic. His friend turned to him and coaxed, "Did you ever see an act as great as that? I ask you, have you ever seen an act like that?"

The cynic shrugged, maintaining his seat, "Aaaah, he's no Heifetz."

38

A French peasant woman goes to the doctor who confirms that she is pregnant. "What is your husband's name?"

"I don't have a husband."

"Who's the father?"

"Pierre the baker."

"Now that you're going to bear his child, why don't you marry him?"

"You're right. I really should."

The following year the scene is repeated, and the doctor says, "You've married Pierre?"

"No, I haven't."

"Really, now. Two children in two years. You really should marry him."

"You're right. I really should."

The following year the scene is again repeated and the doctor inquires, "You took my advice and married Pierre?"

"No."

Now angry, the doctor demands, "Three children in three years! Each time Pierre is the father. Why don't you marry him, for gosh sakes?"

"Gee, I don't know. He just doesn't appeal to me."

39

Two litigants came to the Rabbi and asked him to arbitrate a dispute. The first presented his case, and, upon its culmination, the Rabbi said to him, "You're right!"

The second man, visibly upset, cried, "But Rabbi, you haven't listened to my side of the story."

The Rabbi listened to the second man's story, and, upon its completion, told the second man, "You're right!"

The Rabbi's wife who was standing nearby beckoned to the Rabbi and said to him. "Each of these men comes to you with opposite stories, and after listening to them, how can you come to the conclusion that both are right?"

"You're right, too!" said the Rabbi.

40

A 75-year-old man went to his physician and agitatedly informed the physician that he could no longer perform sexually. The physician was somewhat amused, and inquired, "You're 75 years old, that's not so strange. What upsets you so much?"

The man continued, "Well, it didn't bother me until this week when one of my neighbors in the apartment building who is 80 years old was talking to me. He said that even though he was 80 years old, he could still perform regularly."

The doctor listened to this recital and told the patient, "You say so, too."

41

The senator was facing a tough election battle. There was an important issue which divided his electorate. Half favored the issue; half opposed it. If the senator took sides, he was in big trouble. At the Fourth of July picnic, the senator was called upon to say a few words. When he had completed his speech, a man in the audience questioned, "Say, Senator, how do you stand on this issue?"

"I'm glad you asked. Some of my friends are for this issue. Many of my friends are against this issue. But I'll tell you one thing. For or against, I always stick with my friends."

42

The controller was taking his first airplane flight and, like many controllers, was terrified. The passenger next to him, noticing his discomfort, advised him, "Take it easy. Relax. If it's your time to go, you'll go. If it's not your time to go, you have nothing to worry about."

The controller's anxiety did not abate one bit. He told his fellow passenger, "Yeah, but what if it's the pilot's time to go?"

43

A controller was sharing a foxhole with another G.I. As the shelling began, the controller became terrified and huddled in the foxhole. His fellow G.I. told him, "Take it easy. If one of those shells has got your name on it, you'll go whatever happens. And if one doesn't have your name on it, you're going to be safe."

The controller continued to shake and said, "I'm not concerned about the shells which have my name on them. I'm worried about the ones they send over marked 'To whom it may concern.'"

44

The same group of guys went out on a hunting trip every year, and every year they came back not talking to each other. It seemed that each took turns cooking, and each felt he was being poisoned by the others. Worse still, none of them wanted to do any of the cooking, since each wanted to be free to hunt. This year they made a resolution. Each would take his turn cooking for the day, and anybody who criticized anybody's else's cooking would have to do all the cooking for the rest of the trip. Having all agreed, they left for the hunting grounds.

The first day, all the men but the one assigned to do the cooking went out in the field to hunt. The cook who was left behind decided that after all these years he was finally in a position to get rid of his turn to cook for the rest of the trip. He went into the field, collected horse manure, formed it into patties, and fried them as though they were hamburgers. As the end of the day, the fatigued hunters returned to camp and the cook served them. The first took a bite of his hamburger, spit it out, and sputtered. "Goshamighty! Horse manure! But good, very good!''

45

Two women were arguing or debating the respective merits of their sons. One said, "You know, my son is a doctor. He went to school twelve years, and now he's hung up his shingle, his office is loaded with patients, and he makes himself $50,000 a year.'' The other woman countered with, "Well, my son is a lawyer and he is just a year out of law school. They are breaking down the doors to his office. Already he makes $70,000 a year.''

The first woman came back with, "You should see the big house that my son lives in, a big house out in the suburbs.'' To which the other replied, "My son not only has a big house but he has the largest Cadillac standing in front of it.''

The first woman, not to be outdone, added. "My son, the doctor, he goes to a psychoanalyst, and you know what? He goes three times a week and he pays $75 an hour.'' To which the second woman replied, "So what's so great about that? My son, the lawyer, goes to see a psychoanalyst five times a week. Not only that, he pays $100 an hour—and you know what they talk about? Me!''

46

A noted violinist was being scolded by his manager for his self-adulation. "Every time I see you talking to someone at a cocktail party, you're saying 'I, I, I.'" The violinist, abashed, remarked, "Gee, I didn't know that and I'm sorry. I'll bet I've offended a lot of people that way. I promise I'll never do it again."

The following Sunday, both were at a cocktail party and the violinist was "I, I, I-ing" a friend. Suddenly he looked across the room and saw his manager shaking his head in despair. He gave his manager a sign that he remembered the previous week's promise, turned back to his friend, and said, "But enough talking about me. Let's talk about you. How did you like my last concert?"

47

There's a story that DeGaulle, facing approaching death, wrote the Pope to inquire whether he could be buried under the altar in St. Peter's. He informed the Pope that if he could be granted this honor, he would be willing to make a handsome contribution to the Church. Several days later, DeGaulle received a letter from the Pope in which the Pope indicated that he could be buried under the altar in St. Peter's if he made a contribution of one million dollars. DeGaulle shot back a letter to the Pope, "For only 3 days?"

48

A mother said to a schoolteacher, "My Harold is very sensitive. If ever you must punish him, just slap the boy in the next seat. That will frighten Harold into behaving."

49

A schlemiel is the New York waiter who pours hot soup on the schlemazel.

50

He is such a schlemazel that if it were raining borscht, he'd be caught with a fork.

51

He is such a schlemazel that if they cut a girl in half, he'd get the part that eats (Milton Berle).

52

This schlemazel joins the paratroopers, undergoing physical conditioning, learning how to tumble and fall, pack a parachute, and how to jump from a tower. Finally, he and his group are taken for their first practice jump.

"Here's what we do today," the sergeant instructs. "A plane will take you over the target area. When the light goes on, everyone hooks his chute to the line. Each man will push out the man in front of you, and the line will open your chute automatically. Should your main chute fail to open for some reason, count to three and pull the ring to open your auxiliary chute. When you get down to the ground, a truck will be waiting to take you all back to camp!'

When the plane flies over the jump area, the signal to hook up is given, and the men proceed to jump. Unfortunately, our hero's chute fails to open.

"Thank heaven," he murmurs to himself, "I have an auxiliary chute. One, two, three."

He pulls the ring and to his dismay the ring comes off in his hand. "Damn army!" he mutters as he plummets earthward. "I'll bet when I get down, they won't even have a truck waiting."

53

A schlemiel was feeling depressed and decided to commit suicide by hanging himself. While in the process, a friend came into his room and saw him standing there with a rope around his waist, so he asked him what he was trying to do. The schlemiel answered that he was in the midst of killing himself.

"But if you are killing yourself," asked the friend, "why do you have the rope around your waist?"

"Well," said the man, "when I put the rope around my neck, it began to choke me."

54

There was once a schlemiel who was broke. Charity was available, but he was a proud man and would not accept it. So his friends collected some money and figured out a sure-fire way to convey it to him. They decided to hold a raffle and whoever drew the lucky number from the hat would win. What the schlemiel didn't know was that all the stubs in the hat had his ticket number on it. On the appointed night, the schlemiel was asked to draw the winning number from the hat. He stuck his hand in and pulled out a piece of paper and called out the winning number—"7 1/4."

55

Masochist: "Beat me!"

Sadist: "No."

56

A man was knocked down by a car and only slightly hurt. Nevertheless, he decided to sue the other driver's insurance company for damages. When the court date arrived, the man was carried into court on a stretcher. The jury took one look at him and awarded him a handsome settlement. The investigator for the insurance company was irate, since he knew that the man had not been hurt badly. He walked over to the plaintiff and roared, "I know you're a fraud, so I'm going to tell you my plans. I'm going to put you under surveillance 24 hours a day. You make one false move, and I'll have you back in court for defrauding the insurance company."

The "victim" then asked the insurance investigator. "Would you like to know *my* plans? After I leave this court today, there will be an ambulance at the curb waiting to take me to Kennedy Airport, where I will be boarded on a plane for the overnight trip to Paris. When I arrive in Paris, I will be transferred to a train which will take me to Lourdes. And then, you are going to see the miracle of the century!"

57

An old recluse lived with his cat. Every night he'd let the cat out and the cat would return quickly. When one night the cat didn't return until morning, the irate recluse threatened, "Do that again and I'll have you neutered."

The following night the cat again stayed out all night and the recluse carried out his threat, telling the cat. "Now you'll stay home where you belong."

The following night, much to the recluse's surprise, the cat again stayed out all night. When he returned the next morning, the man inquired, "How come you stayed out all night? You're neutered and can't do anything anyway."

"I know. Now I'm a consultant!"

58

A man drinking at a bar threw the drink in the bartender's face. The bartender drew back his fist to slug him, but before he could deliver the punch, the man apologized profusely and confessed that it was a compulsion, and that he was terribly ashamed of it.

"Why don't you go see a therapist?" the bartender inquired.

"You're right. I will."

Several months later the man returned to the same bar, ordered a drink, and again threw it in the bartender's face. Angrily the bartender thundered, "I thought you were going to see a therapist for that compulsion."

"I did. I still have my compulsion but now I'm not ashamed of my compulsion any longer."

59

Ulcers are not caused by what you eat, but by what's eating you.

60

A young lady comes to see a psychiatrist with a complaint of a persistent itch between her toes. The psychiatrist asks her to remove her stockings so that he may have a look at her toes.

"I don't think that will help," she observes. "The itch is between my two *big* toes."

61

A man insisted to his psychiatrist that he had swallowed a horse. None of the doctor's persuasive tactics could persuade him to change his mind. In desperation, the psychiatrist agreed to "operate." The idea was simply to put the patient under and bring a horse into the operating room.

When the patient came to, the doctor pointed to the horse and said, "Well, that won't worry you any longer." "That's not the horse I swallowed," he said. "That's a bay. My horse was white."

62

A man goes to a psychiatrist and says, "I think I'm going crazy. Every night I see animals, lions, tigers, etc., parading under my bed."

"Okay, lie down on the couch and tell me about it."

"Before I do, how much will it cost me?"

"$50."

"That crazy I'm not," he says as he leaves.

A month later, the psychiatrist sees him on the street and asks how he is.

"My brother-in-law cured me completely in one visit," he answered.

"Oh, is your brother-in-law a psychiatrist?"

"No, he's a carpenter. He cut off the legs of my bed."

63

A mother concerned about her son playing with mudpies decides to visit the psychiatrist. After listening to her, the psychiatrist says, "I don't think you should worry too much just because he makes mudpies."

"You're right, I don't think so either," replied the mother. "It's his wife who is beginning to worry."

64

"Is insanity inherited?"

"Yes, Parents get it from children."

65

Seeing his patient sitting on the hospital lawn, stabbing at the air as if he were catching butterflies, the psychiatrist decided to enter his patient's delusional frame of reference, sat down beside him and began making similar motions. The patient, turning around, looked at the psychiatrist and said, "I'm crazy. What's your excuse?"

66

A patient announced to the psychiatrist on his ward, "Napoleon was my father." The psychiatrist said, "That's interesting." The next day when the psychiatrist came onto the ward, the patient announced, "George Washington was my father." This time the psychiatrist, being a creature of logic, stopped and asked the psychotic patient, "But yesterday you said that Napoleon was your father and today you say George Washington was your father. How do you explain that?"

The psychotic replied, "Different mothers."

67

A novice psychiatrist was seeing his first patient at the mental hospital. When the patient entered and was seated, the psychiatrist asked him why he was in the hospital. The patient answered, "Because I'm dead."

The psychiatrist inquired, "But if you are dead, what are you doing here?"

"Darned if I know. I came home from work this day. I knew I was dead and I told my family to bury me. Instead, they brought me here."

"That's strange. But tell me, do dead people breathe?"

"No, dead people don't breathe."

"Well, you're breathing. How do you explain that?"

"I really can't. *You* explain it."

"Do dead people eat?"

"No, dead people don't eat."

"Well, coming past the dining hall, I just saw you sitting there eating. How do you explain that?"

"*You're* the doctor. If *you* know, why don't *you* tell me?" So the discussion went. The psychiatrist was about to give up when suddenly he had one of those illuminating ideas. He leaned over and asked the patient, "Tell me, do dead people bleed?"

"No dead people don't bleed," replied the patient.

At this point the psychiatrist reached into his desk, took out a long hypodermic needle, and jabbed it into the patient's calf. As he watched the blood run down the patient's leg, the psychiatrist sat back and waited for the patient to admit defeat. The patient looked down at his bleeding calf, looked up, scratched his head, and proclaimed, "By golly! Dead people *do* bleed!!"

68

A man was brought into the ward of a mental hospital screaming at the top of his voice, "I'm Jesus Christ! I'm Jesus Christ!" The attendants could not very easily restrain him. The patients did not know what to make of him. Some dismissed him with a wave of the hand. Others fell on their knees to kiss the hem of his robe. Suddenly an older patient walked over to the screaming new patient, patted him on the shoulder, and soothed him with, "Sit down, my son!"

69

The Swedes and the Norwegians in Minnesota have long had a good natured rivalry. The story goes that this Norwegian couple was making love one night when she stopped him and inquired, "Oley, do the English do this?"

"Of course they do this."

They resumed their lovemaking when again she interrupted with a second inquiry, "Oley, do the French do this?"

"What a question! Of course the French do this!"

They again resumed their lovemaking when she stopped once more and inquired, "Oley, do the Swedes do it?"

"You and your questions! Now, enough! The English do it; the French do it; the Swedes do it."

She leaned over the side of the bed and spat, and said, "Too good for Swedes."

70

Two psychiatrists meet in the hall of their office building. One says to the other one "Good morning" and enters his office.

The other thinks, "I wonder what he meant by that."

71

The student nurse was following the head nurse and the assistant head nurse. As they left a patient's room, the head nurse asked her assistant, "Did you see what I saw when we bathed Mr. Jones? He had the word 'TINY' tattooed on his penis." "I'm so glad you said that because I was beginning to think I was seeing things."

Returning to the nurses' quarters, the student nurse related the incident to the other students who reacted with disbelief. Finally one said, "Let's really find out if it's true. We'll draw straws to see who goes back to the hospital to investigate." So they did, and a gorgeous student nurse drew the short straw. Across to the hospital she went, and when she returned, the others were waiting to get the "true story." "Did he really have the word 'TINY' tattooed on his penis?" "Well, yes and no. He did have a tattoo on his penis but it didn't say 'TINY.' It said 'TICONDEROGA, NY.'"

72

A psychiatrist and a surgeon were out on the golf course on a Wednesday afternoon. The surgeon addressed the psychiatrist, "You know I have a hard job. Many times I hold life and death in my hands. Yet, hard as my job is, I don't envy you yours. How do you stand it, listening to patient's troubles all day?"

"Who listens?"

73

Sign in psychiatrist's office: Satisfaction guaranteed or your mania back.

74

"Did anyone in your family ever suffer from insanity?"

"No, they all enjoyed it!"

75

A farmer is walking down the road when he sees another farmer attempting to move his balking mule. The mule is sitting on his rear end and refusing to move. The farmer who owns the mule pulls from the front end and pushes from the rear, but in vain. The passing farmer, appraising the situation, approaches the first farmer and inquires, "Having trouble with your mule?"

The first farmer replies, "Yup, he won't move no matter what I do." Whereupon, the second farmer asks, "Would you like me to try?"

The first farmer says he would appreciate it if the other man could get him to move. So the second farmer goes into the field and picks up a loose 2x4. Returning, he begins to clout the mule over the head.

The owner of the mule, standing by in horror, exclaims, "I merely wanted you to get my mule to *move*. I didn't want you to *kill* him."

"Sure," answers the second farmer, "I don't plan to kill him. I can get him moving for you, but first I have to get his attention."

76

In an effort to become better acquainted with the children in her class, the teacher asked each child what his/her father did for a living. One answered, "A doctor," another "a salesman," etc. until the teacher reached Johnny. When she asked Johnny the question, he replied, "My father plays the piano in a whorehouse." The teacher was aghast. She commanded, "I want you to bring your father to see me tomorrow."

That evening Johnny informed his father that the teacher wanted to see him. When father inquired as to the nature of the request, Johnny replied that he didn't know why.

The next day, father accompanied Johnny to class. The teacher stepped outside and exclaimed to father, "Yesterday I was asking all the children what their fathers did for a living and when it came to Johnny, he replied that you were...er...ah...a musician...er...ah...in a...er...ah...house of ill repute."

Now it was father's turn to be amazed. He turned to Johnny and demanded, "You know I don't do that. Now why would you tell your teacher a story like that?"

"Well," replied Johnny, "you didn't expect me to tell her you're a psychologist, did you?"

77

This old lady had insomnia, so her family took her to a psychologist who decided to hypnotize her. After placing the woman on the couch, he darkened the room, swung his watch in front of her, and began to recite, "Your eyes are closing. You're falling asleep. Your eyes are closing. You're falling asleep." When it seemed that she was asleep, he left the room and asked the woman's son to watch her. He tiptoed into the room, happy to see his mother finally getting some sleep! Suddenly she opened one eye, nodded to the door, and asked, "The crazy man left already?"

78

One Sunday after church, God and St. Peter went out to the golf course to shoot a round of golf. God teed off first. He took a healthy cut at the ball, the ball ricocheted off a tree and hit a squirrel nearby and stunned it. The dazed squirrel grabbed the ball in his mouth, thinking it was a nut, and ran off with it. As he was running, a hawk was flying above. The hawk swooped down, lifted the squirrel into the air by his neck. The squirrel, in pain, opened his mouth, dropped the ball, and it fell right into the cup. God turned around and looked at St. Peter, who said in disgust, "Now, come on, God. Do you want to screw around or do you want to play golf?"

A neurologist, an orthopedic specialist, and a psychiatrist are walking down Michigan Avenue when they see a man approaching them, walking with a peculiar gait. The neurologist looks at the man, calls the attention of his colleagues to this and says, "There is a classic case of cerebral palsy; look at his scissors gait."

The orthopedic specialist laughs and says, "I guess it's each man to his own specialty, because if you look at this man carefully you will observe that he could not have cerebral palsy; instead, he has ortho-Marie-Strumpfel spine."

The psychiatrist, who has remained quiet until this point, interjects, "The trouble with you people is that whenever you see some physical symptoms, you immediately attach a physical cause to it. Anybody with any psychological background could very easily tell that this man's condition is basically a hysterical manifestation, a camptocormia."

The disagreement increases, and finally the neurologist suggests that they bet ten dollars, stop the man, and ask him. This is agreeable to all three. So, they stop the man and ask him what he is suffering from. The man politely replies, "I'm glad you asked me because I am a physician myself and consequently in a position to give you the true diagnosis. Actually, you are all wrong, because if I don't get to a toilet soon...."

A psychologist working in an army induction station was so overburdened examining new recruits that he had to create a short cut in his examinations. As each prospective draftee came by, the psychologist showed him a blank card and asked him what it reminded him of.

The first draftee indicated that the blank card looked like a field of cotton. The psychologist asked him why it looked like a field of cotton and the draftee said, "I grew up in Alabama and it looks just like the fields when they were full of cotton." The psychologist passed him through.

When it came to the second draftee's turn, the psychologist showed him the blank card, "What does this remind you of?" The draftee replied that it looked like ice. The psychologist asked him, "Why does it look like ice?'' The draftee replied, ''I grew up in Alaska and it looks like glacier ice.'' The psychologist passed him on.

When the third draftee entered, the psychologist showed him the card and asked, ''What does this remind you of?'' The draftee said, ''It reminds me of sex.'' The psychologist said, ''Why does that remind you of sex?'' The draftee replied, *''Everything* reminds me of sex!''

81

A man came to a psychologist for a Rorschach examination. The psychologist showed him Card I and the patient told the psychologist that he saw a penis on it. On Card II, a vagina. On Card III he saw breasts and a penis, and so on through the ten cards. At the end of the testing, the psychologist showed the man to the door. The man turned around and said to the psychologist, ''Before I go, I'm going to a stag party tonight. Can I borrow some of those dirty pictures?''

82

This man went to his doctor, complaining that he felt like he was being suffocated, his eyes bulged, and he had difficulty catching his breath. The doctor examined him and told him that he had six months to live. Given this verdict, he decided to give up his job, move to Florida, and spend his remaining time enjoying life. When he got down to Miami, he went into a clothing store to get himself some summer clothes. The clerk asked him what size shirt he wanted, and he replied that he wanted a size 15 1/2. The clerk looked him over and said, ''I think you ought to take a size 16.'' The man was indignant and exclaimed, ''I've been wearing a size 15 ½ for the last several years. I know my size, and you're not going to sell me another.'' Whereupon the salesman informed him, ''I'll sell you any size you want, but don't blame me if your eyes bulge, you get a strangling feeling in your throat, and you can't catch your breath.''

83

Therapist: ''What did you dream last night?''

Patient: ''I didn't dream anything.''

Therapist: ''How the heck do you expect me to help you if you don't do your homework?''

Two Irishmen meet and one congratulates the other upon his winning the Irish Sweepstakes. "Tell me," says Pat, "How did you select the winning number?"

"It was easy," replies Mike, "It all came to me in a dream."

"In a dream? How did that work?"

"Well, you know, the number that won for me was 57."

"So," says Mike, "you mean you went to bed one night and dreamt the number 57?"

"Oh no!" says Pat. "You know dreams are symbolic and I wouldn't merely dream the number 57."

"Well, what did you dream?"

"Well, I went to sleep this night and suddenly two numbers appeared before me...6 and 9. Since dreams are symbolic, I knew it didn't refer to either 69 or 96 and suddenly right in my dream I had the answer. 6 x 9 = 57."

A man went to see a therapist and complained he had insomnia. The therapist asked him for some details and the man replied, "I just can't sleep. I haven't slept for so long that if I don't get some sleep very soon, I'm going to go mad. I'm a truck driver and every night when I go to sleep, I have this dream in which the phone rings and I'm told I have to drive my truck from here to Cleveland, so I drive the truck to Cleveland and then I drive back. By that time, I'm so tired that when I wake in the morning, I can't meet the day."

The therapist, after listening intently, advised him, "I'll tell you what you might do. If you have that dream again, in the middle of the dream give me a call. I'll come out and share the driving with you. You'll drive one way, I'll drive the other way, and in that way you'll be more rested when you get up in the morning." Then, the therapist told the man to return in a month and tell him how the suggestion worked.

At the next hour, a patient came in with a similar complaint. "Doctor, if I don't get some sleep, I'm going to go mad. It seems every night when I go to sleep I have this dream in which I have to make love to six women. Well, after I've made love to six women, I'm so tired that I have to drag myself out of bed in the morning."

The therapist advised him, "I'll tell you what to do. If you have this dream again, telephone me, and I'll come over, and I'll take care of three of the women for you. That way you won't be so tired in the morning. Come back in a month and tell me how it worked."

A month later, the first man returned and told the therapist, "Doctor, your advice really saved me. Every time I got that dream, I phoned you and you came out and we drove the round trip to Cleveland. Thanks a lot. That was great advice."

He was followed by the second man, who could hardly drag himself into the office. He told the therapist, "It was a terrible month."

The therapist inquired, "Did you take the advice I gave you?"

The patient answered, "I sure did. Every time I had that dream, I phoned you, and every time I got a message from your telephone answering service that you were out driving to Cleveland."

87

Did you hear of the psychiatrist and the proctologist who formed a medical partnership? They specialized in odds and ends.

88

Two GI's were in the barracks on Sunday morning, talking about their exploits the night before. The first asked the second, "Did you have a good time last night?"

The second replied, "Did I have a good time? When 5:00 came, I got into my f— uniform, walked down the road to the f— gate and caught the f— bus into town. When I got to town, I got off the f— bus, and walked into the first f— bar I saw. I walked up to the f— bartender and ordered a f— drink. While I'm standing there drinking my drink, this f— broad walks over and invites me up to her f— apartment. So I go along. We get up to her f— apartment. She takes off all her f— clothes and…''

''Yeah, yeah. What happened then?''

''What do you think happened then? We had sexual intercourse!''

89

The newspaper printed an article about a big holdup which Sgt. Jones had broken up and had arrested all the holdup men. The newspaper article concluded this report with ''Sgt. Jones is a defective on the police force.''

No sooner did the paper hit the stands than Sgt. Jones telephoned the editor saying, ''I'll sue you for libel. You can't write things like that about me, and I want a retraction the same size and same place that the article was today otherwise you'll hear from my attorney.''

The editor attempted to soothe him with, ''You know, that's one of those little gremlins that is running around the composing room and mixes up the type. We certainly had no intentions of offending you. We'll print a retraction tomorrow. Same length, same position in the paper, and we're really dreadfully sorry.''

The next day there's a box in the paper and it says ''Ooops, we goofed. In yesterday's article describing the holdup, we made an unfortunate error in the last paragraph about Sgt. Jones. What we actually intended to say is that Sgt. Jones is a detective on the police farce.''

90

Nine years in a row, when the long winter turned to spring, Mrs. O'Brien emerged from her house, and the neighbors noticed that she was pregnant again. The tenth spring when she came out, no pregnancy. One of her neighbors decided to inquire how come Mrs. O'Brien had broken her string.

''Oh, I owe it all to my new hearing aid.''

''Your new hearing aid?'' ''Yes. You see I'm somewhat deaf and all these years when we'd go to bed, my husband would ask, 'Do you want to go right to sleep or what' and I'd say 'WHAT?'''

Johnny was the neighborhood bad boy. He had a reputation for violence. One day a neighborhood woman came to visit his mother, bringing her little daughter. The two women, wanting to talk undisturbed, sent the children to the downstairs playroom to play. As the mothers talked, one became aware that it was just too quiet downstairs. Johnny's mother went to the top of the basement stairs and called down, "Johnny, what are you doing down there?"

"I'm on top of Mary."

"That's nice, just don't fight!"

92

A little girl who had just moved into a new neighborhood came upon a bunch of the neighborhood kids playing and asked if she could play with them. The girl who was obviously the leader of the group asked her challengingly, "Do you know the facts of life?"

"No. I don't."

"Well, you can't play with us until you know the facts of life."

A few days later, the little girl returned and announced to the leader that she would like to play with them now.

"Do you know the facts of life?"

"Yes, I do!"

"All right. If you're so smart, who made you?"

"Originally or recently?"

93

A man meets his friend coming out of his analyst's office and inquires of him how his analysis is coming.

"Really great," replies the second. "Analysis is really wonderful thing...it really gives you insight into yourself."

"You mean," asks the first, "if Van Gogh had been analyzed, he would not have cut off his ear and sent it to a prostitute?"

"Oh no," says the second, "He still would have done it, but at least he would have known the reason why."

94

A young man has dedicated himself to the career of a loafer. Finally his father gets fed up and tells him, "Tomorrow you go out and look for a job and don't come back until you have one."

That evening the son returns and his father asks, "Do you have a job?"

"Sure, Pop. I was even offered two. One at $100 a week and one at $80."

The suspicious father, knowing his son, asks, "You did take the $100 one?"

"Oh no! I took the $80 one. When I lose the job, why should I lose a hundred-dollar-a-week job?"

95

Three clergymen were discussing the issue of when life begins. The Catholic priest thought it began at conception. The Protestant minister thought it began at birth while the rabbi thought it began when the kids had all grown up and left home and the dog had died.

96

A man sought the services of a prominent analyst, and after detailing his problems, asked the analyst his hourly fee. The analyst replied that his fee was $50.

"I wish I could afford that, but I have a large family and it is difficult as it is to support them. Couldn't you reduce the fee?" So the analyst reduced the fee to $35.

"That's very generous, but $35 is more than I can afford." So the doctor reduced the fee to $25, then to $10, then to $5. When the fee had been settled upon, the perplexed analyst said to the patient, "You know that I'm the most expensive analyst in town. If you couldn't afford it, why did you come to see me?"

"Because," said the patient, "when it comes to my mental health, money is no object."

97

Teacher in a very rich private school: "Okay, that's enough! The next boy who misbehaves will be severely psychoanalyzed."

98

"I don't know why I'm here," the patient explained. "Just because I like pancakes my family thinks I'm crazy and insists I come to see you. Is there anything wrong with liking pancakes?"

"No, there's nothing wrong with that," the therapist agreed. "I like pancakes myself."

"Good! Come over to my house. I have closets full."

99

A man consulted an Adlerian therapist because he felt inferior because of his small stature. After listening to his complaint, the therapist pointed out to him all of the great figures of history who were short but who, nevertheless, lived constructive lives, concluding with "It is not how big you are, but how big you feel inside." The patient, reassured, expressed his gratitude to the therapist and left, walking down the street, feeling nine feet tall....Then a cat ate him.

100

The psychoanalyst was interpreting the young woman's dream. "That," he announced, "is a phallic symbol."

"What's that?"

"It pertains to a phallus."

"I still don't understand."

Unable to explain, he pulled his zipper down, took out his penis, and explained. "That's a phallus."

"Oh, now I understand. It's like a prick, only smaller."

101

A man goes to an Adlerian therapist and after telling him how badly he suffers from inferiority feelings, asks of the therapist, "Do you think I can be cured?"

The therapist replies, "Yes, I do, but then who am *I* to say?"

102

During World War II, a man applied for the job of *shamus* (beadle at the synagogue). The committee found him to be a man of learning, versed in the ways of the synagogue, and decided to hire him. However, when they presented him with the contract, they discovered he could not sign his name. Upon learning this, the committee withdrew the contract reluctantly, for how could the man conduct synagogue business if he could not even sign his name?

This would-be beadle looked for another job, found one in a junk yard, and, selling scrap metal during the war, he made a small fortune. The synagogue was having a fund-raising campaign, and they decided to approach the now-wealthy, one-time applicant for beadle. When they came to his home upon invitation, they discovered the man living in opulence. He offered to make a handsome contribution to the synagogue, for which the committee thanked him profusely. One member of the committee marveled, "Gee, you made all this money and you couldn't even sign your name. Imagine what you could be if you could sign your name!"

"If I could sign my name," responded the rich man, "I'd still be beadle at your synagogue."

103

Mrs. Gotrocks read in the newspaper that the noted portrait painter, Pablo Schwartz, had just arrived in the U.S. as a refugee. On impulse, she telephoned him and asked him if he would do her portrait. He agreed to do so. They negotiated a fee, and he informed her in broken English that he would let her know when he had finished the portrait.

"But one thing I want you to know," she said. "I want the portrait to be representational. None of that surrealistic stuff. I want it to capture the real me. I want it to capture my warmth and social interest."

Several months later the artist telephoned to inform Mrs. Gotrocks that she could come the following Sunday to see the unveiling of her portrait. If she desired, she could bring a few friends. At the appointed time, Mrs. Gotrocks and her friends arrived at the studio, all of them quite excited. The artist drew the veil off the picture. Everyone in the room gasped, for, while the picture looked just like Mrs. Gotrocks, there was what was obviously a male hand sticking down the front of her dress into her bosom.

When Mrs. Gotrocks recovered her composure, she asked, "Why did you put that hand there?"

He replied, "Because you asked me to."

"*I* asked you to?"

"Yes. You know I don't understand English very well. You asked me to paint your portrait to show your social interest. I looked up 'social interest' in the dictionary and it said 'Fellow-feeling in your bosom.'"

104

A couple went to a sex therapist complaining that their sex life had deteriorated. After listening to their communication the therapist suggested that they had made sex too routine an activity and that they ought to inject some spontaneity into their lovemaking, to do it at unexpected times, in unexpected places, and in unexpected ways. When the couple returned the following week, they expressed unlimited gratitude to the therapist.

"That advice you gave us last week," the husband narrated, "was just wonderful. Last Wednesday night we were having dinner when suddenly I had the urge. I put down my knife and fork, moved the dishes aside, bent her back, and we made love right there on the dinner table...Of course, they'll never let us back in Howard Johnson's again."

Client: "Gee, I feel just terrible today."

Nondirective Therapist: "You feel miserable."

Client: "Yes, I'm so upset I don't know what I'm going to do."

Therapist: "You are so upset you can't predict your next move."

Client: "Yes, the future appears so hopeless, about the only thing I can do is kill myself."

Therapist: "You feel so hopeless that you feel the only solution is suicide."

At this point the patient walks over to the window, opens it, and leaps out.

Therapist: "Splat!"

106

The old lady went to the gynecologist for the first time. As the doctor proceeded with the examination, she questioned, "Doctor, does your mother know what you do for a living?"

107

The two new prisoners were assigned to the same cell. The first asked, "How long you in for?"

"Three years."

"What for?"

"Forgery."

The second asked, "How long are you in for?"

"Life."

"What for?"

"Shooting a man in the hand."

"You shot a man in the hand and they gave you life?"

"Yeah, but he was scratching his head at the time."

108

Having completed league bowling for the evening, one bowler suggested to another that they bowl another game. The latter rejected it, saying, "My wife would kill me if I came home late again."

The first man inquired, "What do you do when you go home late?" and the second described his method. "When I'm late, I park my car a block down the street. I walk home ever so quietly, open the door gently, take off my shoes and tiptoe up the stairs. I undress in the dark, get into bed, and she says, 'Out bumming around with your friends again, huh?'"

"No wonder," said the first man. "You have the wrong technique. When I come home late, I drive right up to the door. Before I turn off the ignition, I gun the engine a bit. I open the front door, slam it, and then clomp, clomp up the stairs. I turn on all the lights, get undressed, climb into bed and tell my wife, 'Okay, baby, roll over.' You know what? She's asleep every time."

109

This story is laid in a Swiss mountain town. Despite the warnings of his friends, a villager decides to marry the village shrew. After the wedding, the bride and groom get into a wagon for the descent to their honeymoon cottage in the valley. When they have gone a little way, the horse goes over a bump and jostles the passengers. The bridegroom says, "One!" When they have gone a bit further, the horse gets too close to the edge and, in an effort to compensate, grazes the side of the mountain, almost upsetting the wagon, the bridegroom says, "Two!" As they approach the end of the trip, the descent becomes steep, and the horse begins to travel too fast, again threatening his passengers. After the bridegroom has succeeded in reining in the horse, he alights, says, "Three!" takes out a pistol, and shoots the horse. He carries his bride the remainder of the way to the honeymoon cottage and across the threshold. She takes one look at it, begins to complain, and berates the groom for his poor choice of cottage. The groom, unfazed, says "One!"

A young mother was sitting on a park bench watching her boys frolic in the park. The woman next to her leaned over and said, "My, you have two nice boys. How old are they?"

"Well, the lawyer is three and the doctor is four-and-a-half."

Two Cadillacs pull up in front of a Miami Beach hotel. The first is laden with luggage and the bellboys rush out in anticipation of a large tip. As they are collecting the luggage, the owner of the Cadillac asks the assistant manager whether one of the bellboys could go back to the second car and carry his little boy up to his room. The compassionate assistant manager assigns a bellboy and then says to the father, "I am very sorry that your boy can't walk."

"He *can* walk," says the father, "but thank God I have enough money that he doesn't have to!"

A mother takes her child to the toy department of a large store and the child runs about playing with all the toys. When the mother is through with her own shopping, she comes to retrieve the child, who is sitting on a rocking horse. She asks the child to leave with her, but he kicks up a fuss. The poor mother is embarrassed and is helpless in the face of her child's unwillingness to get off the horse.

The department manager, seeing the commotion, asks the mother what the difficulty is. When the mother explains to him, he says, "Well, that's no trouble at all....it so happens we have a psychologist on the staff of our store. I will call him down and ask him to help you get the boy off the horse."

The psychologist, being summoned, walks over to the boy and whispers something in his ear, and immediately the little boy gets off the horse and runs to his mother begging, "Please, mommy, take me home." The mother is quite agreeable but asks the boy to wait a minute, and then walks over and asks the psychologist, "Gee, those were amazing results...I wish you would tell me how you did it so that I will be able to handle these situations myself later."

"Simple," says the psychologist, "I just walked over and said, 'Listen, you little S.O.B., get off that horse before I beat your ears in,'' and off he got."

113

Psychiatrists never punish their children. Being the child of a psychiatrist is punishment enough.

114

First mother: "My child started to walk when he was 10 months old. How old was your child when he began to walk?"

Second mother: "I really don't know. You see, I'm raising him, not racing him."

115

Running into the kitchen breathlessly, Jimmy demanded of his mother, "Hey, Mom, where did I come from?" His mother, who had been reading all the manuals on child rearing, went into a long detailed description of anatomy, the sexual act, and birth. When she completed her narration, she noticed Jimmy standing there scratching his head. "Jimmy, is there something you don't understand?"

"Yeah, Mom. I just talked to Tommy, and he said he came from Pennsylvania."

116

A boy and his father are taking a walk when suddenly a large dog bounds from the bushes barking vigorously. The boy hides behind his father trembling. His father reaches around,pats the boy on the head, and says, "You can come out. Everyone knows that barking dogs don't bite."

The boy is not placated. "*You* know that and *I* know it, but does the dog know it?"

117

What is the difference between a diplomat and a lady?

When a diplomat says "yes," he means "maybe."

When he says "maybe," he really means no."

But if he says "no," he wouldn't be a diplomat.

A lady, when she says "no," means "maybe."

When she says "maybe," she really means "yes."

But were she to say "yes," she'd be no lady.

118

Three clients are sitting in an Adlerian psychologist's office and comparing notes. The first one says, "He asked for my early recollections last week. Do you know how far back I could remember? I could remember lying in my cradle watching the crib toy hanging overhead."

The second said, "That's remembering pretty far back, but I can remember even further. When he asked me about my early recollections, I told him about how I was born. I remember coming down the birth canal and then suddenly being wrenched away from my mother and then the doctor paddling me."

The third said, "Both of you can certainly remember way back, but I can remember even further back than that. I remember going to a picnic with my father and coming home with my mother."

119

The psychologist was addressing the pessimists' convention. He started his address by announcing, "Ladies and gentlemen, I have some good news and some bad news. First, I'd like to tell you the good news—I have some bad news for you!"

120

Clancy had not been feeling well, and went to consult the doctor. "It's your heart," said the doctor, "You'll just have to stop drinking or else...." To Clancy this was almost the equivalent of a death sentence, since every day for twenty years he had stopped off at his favorite tavern after work and had had a few belts with the boys before going home to dinner. It was his whole social life.

The following day, Clancy got off the bus, and as he passed the tavern his feet began to turn in. Clancy stopped himself just in time and reminded himself, "Now, Clancy, you remember what the doctor said. Turn around and go home." Clancy turned around and headed toward home, but as he got a few steps past the tavern, it occurred to him that the doctor did not say that Clancy could not look through the window to see who was at the bar. Clancy turned around and did just that and through the window he could see his friends whooping it up. Clancy then said to himself, "Now come on, Clancy, you're tearing your heart out. Turn around and go home." Clancy turned around and walked home again. When he got to the corner, the light was red, and Clancy stopped. As he was standing there waiting for the light to turn green, a thought ran through Clancy's head. "Clancy, you're wonderful! Imagine that! After twenty years drinking with the boys day in and day out, you're able to turn around and go home. That's real will power! By golly, will power like that deserves a drink!" and back to the bar he headed.

121

Mr. Brown received his check on Friday and found he was $5.00 short in paying his bills. He went to Mr. White and asked Mr. White for a loan of $5.00 until the following Friday, which was payday. Mr. White agreed and gave him the $5.00. When the following Friday arrived, Mr. Brown found that he was still $5.00 short, but, since he had made a promise to pay Mr. White that day, he went to his friend Mr. Green and asked him for $5.00 on the same terms that he had previously agreed to with Mr. White. He took the $5.00 from Mr. Green and gave it to Mr. White, and the following Friday Mr. Brown found himself $5.00 short again. He went to Mr. White and said to him, "A few weeks ago, I borrowed $5.00 from you. I was good as my word and returned the money on time. Now, since you know me to be a man who pays his debts, would you lend me $5.00 again?" Mr. White, of course, did. Mr. Brown took that $5.00 and gave it to Mr. Green. So it went from Friday to Friday. One Friday he borrowed from Mr. Green to pay Mr. White, and the following Friday he borrowed from Mr. White to pay Mr. Green. Finally Mr. Brown just got tired of running back and forth every Friday. So he called his creditors together and explained the situation to them, and finished with, "I'm tired from running back and forth, and it seems like I will never have enough money to get out of this bind, so why don't the two of you do me a favor? Next Friday, you, Mr. Green, send $5.00 to Mr. White. The following Friday, Mr. White, you send $5.00 to Mr. Green, and please, the both of you leave me out of it.''

122

This mouse who made her home in a hole in the wall in the psychology laboratory at the university had taken her two children for a walk through the laboratory. As they were returning to the hole, the mother noticed that a cat was blocking the entrance. The baby mice were terrified, but the mother was not dismayed. She looked the cat straight in the eye and said, ''Rufff!'' The cat turned tail and ran. The mother mouse turned to her children and said, ''That's a lesson for you. It never hurts to know a second language.''

123

Two men were exchanging complaints about their respective wives. One was saying, ''My wife is terrible. She just doesn't know what to do with money. On Sunday, she came up to me and said, 'Give me $10.' I asked her, 'What do you need $10 for?' She said that it was none of my business, that I could either give her the $10 or not give her the $10. On Monday, she's back and asks me for $25. I asked her, 'What do you need with $25?' She answered, 'Why must you always check up on me? Either give me the $25 or don't give me the $25, but don't ask me so many questions.' On Tuesday, she's back and asking me for $50. So, again I asked her, 'What do you need with $50?' And, again, the same answer: It was none of my business. I could give her the $50 or not.''

The other man said to the first, ''What could she do with all that money?''

To which the other man replied, ''How should I know? Do you think I give it to her?''

124

A little boy who was six years old had not spoken a word all the six years of his life. This day he was sitting, eating his dinner, when suddenly he spit out his soup and sputtered, ''Gee that soup's terrible!''

His startled mother exclaimed, ''You can talk! You can talk!''

"Of course I can talk."

"Then why haven't you talked until now?"

"Until now I liked the way you made the soup."

125

There were once two brothers, one good and one bad. The good brother lived a virtuous life, while the bad brother engaged in a life of debauchery. At the same time, the bad brother prospered while the good brother was as poor as a churchmouse. Nevertheless, the good brother consoled himself with the thought that when the time came for them to go to their reward, he would go to heaven and his wicked brother would unfortunately go to the other place. The bad brother died and his good brother mourned him, all the while regretting the fact that his brother's conduct in life must surely have earned him a trip to Hell.

Several years later the good brother died and, sure enough, just as he had been told, he found himself in front of the Pearly Gates with St. Peter waiting to greet him. St. Peter greeted him warmly, led him inside, and took him over to the supply shop to be outfitted with a toga and wings and a halo. Then over to the music shop for a harp, and finally over to the motor pool for a cloud. Having been thus supplied, he was told by St. Peter, "You've lived a good life. Now enjoy Heaven!"

The good brother cruised around Heaven on his cloud, enjoying it all. Maybe he hadn't had it so good on earth, but it was all worth it. As he sat on his cloud strumming on his harp, he noticed a Cadillac-sized cloud floating by, and who should be on it but his no-good brother? To add insult to injury, his brother had one arm around a blonde and the other around a keg of whiskey. The good brother was dismayed, flew back to St. Peter, and protested, "It's not fair! It's not fair! I lived a good life and I got a halo, a harp, and a small cloud, and there's my no-good brother, who never did a good thing in his life, and he has a tremendous cloud, a blond, and a keg of whiskey. It's just not fair!"

St. Peter soothed the good brother and observed, "If you had looked closer, you wouldn't be so upset. You would have noticed that the keg of whiskey had a hole in it and the blonde didn't."

A nonconforming song sparrow decided not to fly South for the winter. Weeks passed and the cold drove the bird from his nest. As he flew, ice began to form on his wings and he crashed safely into a barnyard. A cow wandered by and crapped on the dazed bird. The sparrow thought his end had come but instead the cow manure warmed him. His wings defrosted and he even had some lunch. Warm and happy, the little bird began to sing. A cat happened through the barnyard and, hearing the singing, investigated the pile of manure. The cat found the happy sparrow and promptly ate him.

The story has three morals:

1. Everyone who dumps shit on you is not necessarily your enemy.

2. Anyone who takes shit off you is not necessarily your friend.

3. If you are full of shit...keep your mouth shut!

A man sued the railroad company for injuries he sustained when his car was struck by a train at the crossing. Called upon to testify, the railroad guard indicated that when the train passed through, he had been standing at the crossing, waving his lantern and that the plaintiff had nevertheless ignored the warning and crossed the tracks. The jury awarded the plaintiff no damages. After the hearing the watchman's assistant pointed out to the watchman that he had forgotten to testify that the lantern had not been lit, to which the watchman replied, "But no one asked me that."

A father and his little boy were walking down the street when the little boy noticed two dogs sexually engaged.

"What are those doggies doing?" asked the boy.

"Well, the dog in back hurt his legs and the dog in front is carrying him to the hospital."

"Well, it just goes to show you what life is like. You try to help someone and he'll screw you every time."

129

Anyone who goes to see a psychiatrist ought to have his head examined (Sam Goldwyn).

130

The hospitalized patient complained, "The food here is so lousy and such small portions besides."

131

He is such a hypochondriac that whenever he gets a pimple on his behind, he thinks that he has a brain tumor.

132

A little boy is referred to a child psychologist because he compulsively snaps his fingers. The psychologist inquires why he does it, and the boy replies, "Because it keeps the zebras away."

"But there are no zebras in the United States. They're all in Africa, thousands of miles away."

"See what I mean?"

133

Husband: "Here are two aspirin."

Wife: "Why are you giving me aspirin? I don't have a headache."

Husband: "Good! Let's go to bed."

134

A teenage girl goes into Marshall Field's and looks at the dresses. She finally finds one she likes and the clerk begins to wrap it. At that point the girl has second thoughts, stops the clerk, and inquires, "If I take it home and my mother likes it, can I return it?"

135

A fox foraging in the forest finds it difficult to find any food. Nearly starving he decides to go into town and forage for food. After dark he skulks into town. He is so hungry that crossing the railroad tracks, he forgets to look and a train bears down on him, runs over his tail, and amputates it. The fox leaps into the air, yelping with pain. As he comes down to earth, he turns around to see what happened to him. Because he is in such pain, he again forgets to look, and a train, passing in the opposite direction decapitates him. The moral of this story is "Never lose your head over a piece of tail!"

136

Trying to influence your child with your voice is like trying to steer your car with the horn (Rudolf Dreikurs).

137

"How many psychiatrists does it take to change a light bulb?"

"One, but only if it wants to change."

138

A drunk walking through the park, notices a man doing pushups, and inquires, "What'samatter? Lose your girl?"

139

An American in Paris is using the *pissoir* when he is approached by a Frenchman. "Mon Dieu," says the stranger, "I have never seen such magnificent genitalia. Couldn't I hold them for just a moment? They're superb and beautiful!" The American did not know how to respond to this request and finally responded with, "OK, just for a second, and then get out of here." The stranger then closed one hand around the man's testicles and reaching out with the other hand, said calmly, "And now, monsieur, give me your wallet."[18]

---

[18]Mosak and Gushurst (1971) used this story as an admonition to therapists not to succumb to patient flattery.

"You want to know how to catch an elephant? You dig a pit in the jungle large enough to contain an elephant and you line it with cinders. Then you hide in the bushes. Pretty soon a curious elephant will appear and look over the edge of the pit. Then you leap out of the bushes and kick him in the ashhole."

141

"You want to know how to catch an elephant? You have to have a telescope, a matchbox, and a tweezer. When you see an elephant coming, you hold the telescope up to your eye the wrong way. That will make the elephant small. So you pick him up with the tweezer, put him into the matchbox, and close it."

142

The President of France came to the U.S. for a state visit. While one group of reporters was interviewing him at the airport, another group was interviewing his wife. One asked her, "What is the most important thing in life?" "A penis," she replied.

Her husband turned to her and snapped, "How many times must I tell you it's pronounced ''appiness'?"

143

A group of fellows are engaged in their regular poker game. One gets four aces, bets all of his money, and loses to a straight flush. As the other rakes in the money, he drops dead. Now the question is who will tell his wife. They draw cards, and the man with the lowest card now has to break the news. He goes over to her house, and when the unwitting widow opens the door, he blurts out, "Your husband lost $1,000 in the poker game tonight!"

"$1,000? He should drop dead!"

"He did!"

144

A horse appears at spring training camp and asks Casey Stengel for a tryout. The other players laugh, but Casey Stengel decides to give him a tryout. The horse takes a bat, goes up to the plate, and Whitey Ford throws a pitch to him. The horse promptly hits it over the fence. Ford throws another pitch and again the horse lines it over the fence. Stengel offers him a contract. It's now the first day of the season at Yankee Stadium. The Yankees are behind by a run in the ninth inning. With a man on base, the horse comes to bat as a pinch hitter. The opposing pitcher throws one, and the horse hits it up against the fence. The crowd is going out of its mind until they notice that the horse is not running to first. Stengel is dancing up and down, and yelling at the horse, "Run, dammit, run!" The horse turns to Stengel and announces, "If I could run, I'd be at Hialeah!"

145

A Texan is wandering around the Negev desert in Israel. It being very hot, he stops at a ranch house and asks the rancher for a drink of water. While drinking the water, he observes, "This is a nice ranch you have here. But down in Texas, I get up in the morning and I get into my Jeep and I drive and by nightfall I still haven't reached the fence."

The Israeli rancher observes, "Yeah, I once had a Jeep like that, too."

146

Mr. Goldberg is taking his first trans-Atlantic liner trip and is assigned to a table for dinner. At dinner his partner, a Frenchman, arrives, clicks his heels and says, "*Bon appetit.*" Mr. Goldberg thinking that this is the Frenchman's name, rises, clicks his heels and says, "Goldberg." This goes on for three or four days and finally Mr. Goldberg tells another passenger of this interplay. The other passenger explains to Goldberg that the Frenchman is wishing him a hearty appetite and that "*Bon appetit*" is not his name. This leaves Mr. Goldberg red-faced. That evening when the Frenchman arrives for dinner, Goldberg rises and exclaims, "*Bon appetit!*"

The Frenchman clicks his heels and exclaims, "Goldberg!"

A young assistant in the produce department of a supermarket in Tulsa is confronted by a large strapping Texan who wants to buy half a head of lettuce. The assistant, thinking this is an outrageous request, excuses himself, walks over to his manager, and complains, "There's a crazy guy out there that wants to buy a half head of lettuce," and as the words leave his mouth, he notices that the Texan is standing right behind him. So, he continues with, "so I'm going to sell the other half to this fine gentleman here."

After the sale is rung up, the manager says to his assistant, "Wow! That was quick thinking. I thought he'd kill you. You are really able to think quickly on your feet and our supermarket chain needs people like you to be managers. How would you like it if I recommended you for an opening in Detroit?"

"Detroit? All they have in Detroit are whores and hockey players."

"I'll have you know that my wife comes from Detroit."

"Really? What team does she play for?"

148

Mrs. Flaherty and Mrs. Dugan are talking over the back fence and Mrs. Flaherty is complaining about her husband who comes home drunk and then wets the bed during his sleep. Mrs. Dugan tells her that her child was a bed wetter but that she cured him of his bed wetting by tying a string around his penis. That night his wife undresses him and puts him to bed. Remembering Mrs. Dugan's advice, she searches for a piece of string, and unable to find one she takes a piece of blue ribbon out of her sewing kit and ties it around Paddy's penis. The following morning a hung-over Paddy awakens, looks through bloodshot eyes, and exclaims, "I don't know where I was last night and I don't know what I did, but I sure took first prize at it."

149

A woman is walking with her little girl along the beach near the ocean when suddenly a large wave races across the beach and carries the little girl into the ocean. The distraught mother begins to pray, "Dear

God. Please bring my little girl back and I will serve you forever.'' At that moment another large wave washes her out onto the sands. Her mother grasps her to her bosom but remembers to thank God and then taking a closer look at her daughter, "She was wearing a hat. Where is it?''

150

Psychiatry enables us to correct our faults by confessing our parents' shortcomings. (Joey Adams)

REFERENCES

REFERENCES

Adelson, J. (1974). The dreams of creative college girls. In R.L. Woods and H.B. Greenhouse (Eds.), *The new world of dreams* (pp. 17-21). New York: Macmillan.

Adler, A. (1927a). *The practice and theory of Individual Psychology*. New York: Harcourt, Brace.

Adler, A. (1927b). *Understanding human nature*. New York: Greenberg.

Adler, A. (1958). *What life should mean to you*. New York: Capricorn Books.

Adler, A. (1963). The problem of distance. In A. Adler, *The practice and theory of Individual Psychology* (pp. 100-108). Paterson, NJ: Littlefield, Adams.

Adler, A. (1964a). *Problems of neurosis*. New York: Harper Torchbooks.

Adler, A. (1964b). *Social interest: A challenge to mankind*. New York: Capricorn Books.

Allen, S. (1972). The uses of comedy. *Journal of Creative Behavior, 6,* 83-85.

Ansbacher, H.L. (1965). *Sensus privatus versus sensus communis. Journal of Individual Psychology, 21,* 48-50.

Ansbacher, H.L., & Ansbacher, R.R. (Eds.). (1956). *The Individual Psychology of Alfred Adler*. New York: Basic Books.

Ansbacher, H.L., & Ansbacher, R.R. (Eds.). (1964). *Superiority and social interest*. New York: Viking Press.

Ansell, C., Mindess, H., Stern, E.M., & Stern, V.F. (1981). Pies in the face and similar matters. *Voices, 16(4),* 10-23.

Arnez, N.L., & Anthony, C.B. (1968). Contemporary Negro humor as social satire. *Phylon, 29,* 339-346.

Asimov, I. (1971). *Isaac Asimov's treasury of humor*. Boston: Houghton Mifflin.

Averill, J.R. (1969). Autonomic response patterns during sadness and mirth. *Psychophysiology, 5,* 399-414.

Baron, R.A., & Bell, R.L. (1974). The aggression-inhibiting influence of non-hostile humor. *Journal of Experimental Social Psychology, 10,* 22-33.

Berkowitz, L. (1970). Aggressive humor as a stimulus to aggressive responses. *Journal of Personality and Social Psychology, 16,* 710-717.

Berlyne, D.E. (1972). Humor and its kin. In J.H. Goldstein and P.E. McGhee (Eds.), *The psychology of humor* (pp. 43-60). New York: Academic Press.

Berne, E. (1964). *Games people play*. New York: Grove Press.

Bonime, W. (1962). *The clinical use of dreams*. New York: Basic Books.

Brenner, C. (1955). *Elements of psychoanalysis*. New York: Doubleday Anchor.

Brody, M.W. (1950). The meaning of laughter. *Psychoanalytic Quarterly, 19,* 192-201.

Buckham, J.W. (1946). Humor at a time like this. *Personalist, 27,* 413-424.

Burma, J.H. (1946). Humor as a technique in race conflict. *American Sociological Review, 11,* 710-715.

Burton, R. (1932). *Anatomy of melancholy*. New York: Dutton. (Original work published 1612)

Byrne, D. (1956). The relationship between humor and the expression of hositility. *Journal of Abnormal and Social Psychology, 53,* 84-89.

Byrne, D., Terrill, J., & McReynolds, P. (1962). Incongruency as a predictor of response to humor. *Journal of Abnormal and Social Psychology, 62,* 435-438.

Carter, B. with Greenberg, P.S. (1976, March 1). A ray of sunshine. *Newsweek*.

Cassell, J.I. (1974). The function of humor in the consulting process. *Rehabilitation Counseling Bulletin, 17,* 240-245.

Chapman, A.J. (1975). Humorous laughter in children. *Journal of Personality and Social Psychology, 31,* 42-49.

Coser, R.L. (1959). Some social functions of laughter: A study of humor in a hospital setting. *Human Relations, 12,* 171-181.

Cousins, N. (1979). *Anatomy of an illness*. New York: Norton.

Csikszentmihalyi, M. (1975). *Beyond boredom and anxiety*. San Francisco: Jossey-Bass.

Cupchik, G.C., & Levanthal, H. (1974). Consistency between expressive behavior and the elevation of humorous stimuli. *Journal of Personality and Social Psychology, 30,* 429-442.

Dailey, C. (1966). The experimental study of clinical guessing. *Journal of Individual Psychology, 22,* 65-79.

Darwin, C. (1965). *The expression of emotions in man and animals*. Chicago: University of Chicago Press.

Dreikurs, R. (1951). How does humor affect our lives? *Northwestern Reviewing Stand, 17(10),* 3-9.

Dreikurs, R. (1964). *Children: The challenge*. New York: Hawthorn Books.

Dreikurs, R. (1971). *Social equality: The challenge of today*. Chicago: Regnery.

Dreikurs, R. (1974). The private logic. In H.H. Mosak (Ed.), *Alfred Adler: His influence on psychology today* (pp. 19-32). Park Ridge, NJ: Noyes Press.

Dreikurs, R., Corsini, R., Lowe, R., & Sonstegard, M. (Eds.). (1959). *Adlerian family counseling: A manual for counseling centers.* Eugene, OR: University of Oregon Press.

Dworkin, E.S., & Efran, J.S. (1967). The angered: Their susceptibility to varieties of humor. *Journal of Personality and Social Psychology, 6,* 233-236.

Eibl-Eibesfeldt, I. (1970). *Ethology: The biology of behavior.* New York: Holt, Rinehart & Winston.

Ellenberger, H. (1970). *The discovery of the unconscious.* New York: Basic Books.

Ellis, A. (1977). Fun as psychotherapy. *Rational Living, 12(1),* 2-6.

Ellis, A. (1981). The use of rational humorous songs in psychotherapy. *Voices, 16(4),* 29-36.

Fadiman, C. (1972). Humor as a weapon. *Journal of Creative Behavior, 6,* 87-92.

Farrelly, F., & Brandsma, J. (1974). *Provocative psychotherapy.* Millbrae, CA: Celestial Arts.

Ferris, D.R. (1972). Humor and creativity: Research and theory. *Journal of Creative Behavior, 6,* 75-79.

Frankl, V.E. (1969). *The will to meaning.* New York: New American Library.

Freedman, D.G. (1964). Smiling in blind infants and the issue of innate vs. acquired. *Journal of Child Psychology and Psychiatry, 5,* 171-184.

Freud, S. (1960). *Jokes and their relation to the unconscious.* New York: Norton.

Fried, E. (1970). *Active/Passive: The crucial psychological dimension.* New York: Grune and Stratton.

Fromm, E. (1951). *The forgotten language.* New York: Grove Press.

Gardner, R.A. (1971). *Therapeutic communication with children: Mutual story-telling technique.* New York: Science House.

Getzels, J.W., & Jackson, P.W. (1962). *Creativity and intelligence.* New York: John Wiley.

Goldstein, J.H., Suls, J.M., & Anthony, S. (1972). Enjoyment of specific types of humor content: Motivation or salience? In J.H. Goldstein and P.E. McGhee (Eds.), *The psychology of humor* (pp. 159-172). New York: Academic Press.

Goodchilds, J.D. (1972). On being witty: Causes, correlates, and consequences. In J.H. Goldstein and P.E. McGhee (Eds.), *The psychology of humor* (pp. 173-193). New York: Academic Press.

Goodchilds, J.D., & Smith, E.D. (1964). The wit and his group. *Human Relations, 17,* 23-31.

Goodrich, A.T., Henry, J., & Goodrich, D.W. (1954). Laughter in psychiatric staff conferences: A sociopsychiatric analysis. *American Journal of Orthopsychiatry, 24,* 175-184.

Graham, L.R. (1958). The maturational factor in humor. *Journal of Clinical Psychology, 14,* 326-328.

Gray, D.J. (1966). Uses of Victorian laughter. *Victorian Studies, 10,* 145-176.

Greenwald, H. (1967). Play therapy for children over twenty-one. *Psychotherapy, 4,* 44-46.

Greenwald, H. (1975). Humor in psychotherapy. *Journal of Contemporary Psychotherapy, 7,* 113-116.

Grossman, S.A. (1970). The use of sexual jokes in psychotherapy. *Medical Aspects of Human Sexuality, 4,* 35-46.

Grossman, S.A. (1977). The use of jokes in psychotherapy. In A. Chapman and H.C. Foot (Eds.), *It's a funny thing, humour* (pp. 144-153). Oxford, UK: Pergamon.

Grotjahn, M. (1949). Laughter in psychoanalysis. *Samiksa, 3,* 76-82.

Grotjahn, M. (1966). *Beyond laughter: Humor and the subconscious.* New York: McGraw-Hill.

Grotjahn, M. (1971). Laughter in group psychotherapy. *International Journal of Group Psychotherapy, 21,* 234-238.

Grotjahn, M. (1972). Sexuality and humor: Don't laugh! *Psychology Today, 6,* 51-53.

Hahn, J. (1972). The art of seeming. In P. Adams (Ed.), *Humane social psychiatry* (pp. 141-152). Gainesville, FL: Tree of Life Press.

Hall, G.S., & Allin, A. (1897). The psychology of tickling, laughing, and the comic. *American Journal of Psychology, 8,* 1-41.

Hassett, J., & Houlihan, J. (1979). Different jokes for different folks. *Psychology Today, 12*(8), 64-71.

Hassett, J., & Schwartz, G.E. (1977, February 1). Why can't people take humor seriously? *New York Times Magazine, 103.*

Hauck, W.E., & Thomas, J.W. (1972). The relationship of humor to intelligence, creativity, and intentional and incidental learning. *Journal of Experimental Education, 40,* 52-55.

Jason, H. (1967). The Jewish joke: The problem of definition. *Southern Folklore Quarterly, 31,* 48-54.

Kadis, A.L., & Winick, C. (1973). The cartoon as therapeutic catalyst. In H.H. Mosak (Ed.), *Alfred Adler: His influence on psychology today* (pp. 106-123). Park Ridge, NJ: Noyes Press.

Kass, M. (1967, August 13). What's so funny and why? *Houston Post.*

Keith-Spiegel, P. (1972). Early conceptions of humor: Varieties and issues. In J.H. Goldstein and P.E. McGhee (Eds.), *The psychology of humor* (pp. 4-39). New York: Academic Press.

Kelling, G.W. (1971). An empirical investigation of Freud's theory of jokes. *Psychoanalytic Review, 58,* 473-485.

Koestler, A. (1980). *Brickbats to Babel.* New York: Random House.

Kubie, L.S. (1971). The destructive potential of humor in psychotherapy. *American Journal of Psychiatry, 127,* 861-866.

Kuhlman, T.L. (1984). *Humor and psychotherapy.* Homewood, IL: Dow Jones-Irwin.

Lathrop, D.D. (1981). Laughing away the CIA (and other paranoid delusions). *Voices, 16(4),* 7-9.

Lazarsfeld, S. (1966). The courage for imperfection. *Journal of Individual Psychology, 22,* 163-165. (Original work published 1927)

Leak, G.K. (1974). Effects of hostility arousal and aggressive humor on catharsis and humor preference. *Journal of Personality and Social Psychology, 30,* 736-740.

Lefcourt, H.M., Sordoni, C., & Sordoni, C. (1974). Locus of control and the expression of humor. *Journal of Personality, 42,* 130-143.

Lenzberg, K. (1937). Concerning wit and humor. *International Journal of Individual Psychology, 3(1),* 81-87.

Le Shan, E. (1982). *On living your life.* New York: Harper & Row.

Levine, J., & Abelson, R. (1959). Humor as a disturbing stimulus. *Journal of General Psychology, 60,* 191-200.

Levine, J., & Rakusin, J. (1959). The sense of humor of college students and psychiatric patients. *Journal of General Psychology, 60,* 183-190.

Levine, J., & Redlich, F.C. (1960). Intellectual and emotional factors in the appreciation of humor. *Journal of General Psychology, 62,* 25-35.

Lifschitz, M. (1981). Humor and healing. *Voices, 16(4),* 78-79.

Lundberg, C.C. (1969). Person-focused joking: Pattern and function. *Human Organization, 28,* 22-28.

Manaster, G.J., Painter, G., Deutsch, D., & Overholt, B.J. (1977). *Alfred Adler: As we remember him.* Chicago: North American Society of Adlerian Psychology.

Marcus, N.N. (1969). A psychotherapeutic corroboration of the meaning of the smiling response. *Psychoanalytic Review, 56,* 387-401.

Martineau, W.H. (1972). A model of the social functions of humor. In J.H. Goldstein and P.E. McGhee (Eds.), *The psychology of humor* (pp. 101-125). New York: Academic Press.

McGhee, P.E. (1972a). Methodological and theoretical considerations for a cross-cultural investigation of children's humor. *International Journal of Psychology, 7,* 13-21.

McGhee, P.E. (1972b). On the cognitive origins of incongruity humor: Fantasy assimilation versus reality assimilation. In J.H. Goldstein & P.E. McGhee (Eds.), *The psychology of humor* (pp. 61-80). New York: Academic Press.

McGhee, P.E. (1979). *Humor: Its origin and development.* San Francisco: W.H. Freeman.

Mead, G.H. (1934). *Mind, self, and society.* Chicago: University of Chicago Press.

Meerloo, J.A.M. (1966). The biology of laughter. *Psychoanalytic Review, 53,* 25-44.

Mettee, D.R., Hrelec, E.S., & Wilkins, P.C. (1971). Humor as an interpersonal asset and liability. *Journal of Social Psychology, 85,* 51-64.

Mettee, D.R., & Wilkins, P.C. (1972). When similarity "hurts": Effects of perceived ability and a humorous blunder on interpersonal attractiveness. *Journal of Personality and Social Psychology, 22,* 246-258.

Moody, R.A., Jr. (1978). *Laugh after laugh: The healing power of humor.* Jacksonville, FL: Headwaters Press.

Mosak, H.H. (1958). Early recollections as a projective technique. *Journal of Projective Techniques, 22,* 302-311.

Mosak, H.H. (1968). The interrelatedness of the neuroses through central themes. *Journal of Individual Psychology, 24,* 67-70.

Mosak, H.H. (1972). Lifestyle. In A.G. Nikelly (Ed.), *Techniques for behavior change* (pp. 77-81). Springfield, IL: C.C. Thomas.

Mosak, H.H. (1973). The controller: A social interpretation of the anal character. In H.H. Mosak (Ed.), *Alfred Adler: His influence on psychology today* (pp. 43-52). Park Ridge, NJ: Noyes Press.

Mosak, H.H. (1983). A range of comments on homosexuality and Kivel's article. *Individual Psychology, 39(1),* 222-236.

Mosak, H.H. (1984). Adlerian psychotherapy. In R.J. Corsini (Ed.), *Current psychotherapies* (3rd ed.) (pp. 56-107). Itasca, IL: F.E. Peacock.

Mosak, H.H., & Gushurst, R.S. (1971). What patients say and what they mean. *American Journal of Psychotherapy, 25,* 428-436.

Mosak, H.H., & Mosak, B. (1978). Mutual respect. *Individual Psychologist, 15(3),* 12-14.

Mosak, H.H., & Phillips, K.S. (1980). *Demons, germs and values.* Chicago: Alfred Adler Institute.

Mosak, H.H., & Schneider, S. (1977). Masculine protest, penis envy, women's liberation and sexual equality. *Journal of Individual Psychology, 33(2),* 193-202.

Mosak, H.H., & Shulman, B.H. (1974). *Individual psychotherapy: A syllabus.* Chicago: Alfred Adler Institute.

Murphy, B., & Pollio, H.R. (1973). I'll laugh if you will. *Psychology Today, 7,* 106-110.

Narboe, N. (1981). Why did the therapist cross the road? *Voices, 16*(4), 55-58.

Nikelly, A.G. (Ed.). (1971). *Techniques for behavior change.* Springfield, IL: C.C. Thomas.

Nosanchuk, T.A., & Lightstone, J. (1974). Canned laughter and public and private conformity. *Journal of Personality and Social Psychology, 29,* 153-156.

O'Connell, W.E. (1960). The adaptive functions of wit and humor. *Journal of Abnormal and Social Psychology, 61,* 263-270.

O'Connell, W.E. (1964). Resignation, humor and wit. *Psychoanalytic Review, 51,* 49-56.

O'Connell, W.E. (1966). The humor of the gallows. *Omega, 1,* 32-33.

O'Connell, W.E. (1972). Frankl, Adler, and spirituality. *Journal of Religion and Health, 2,* 134-138.

O'Connell, W.E. (1975). The humorous attitude: Research and clinical beginnings. In W.E. O'Connell (Ed.), *Action therapy and Adlerian therapy,* pp. 183-197. Chicago: Alfred Adler Institute.

O'Connell, W.E., & Peterson, P. (1964). Humor and repression. *Journal of Existentialism, 4,* 309-316.

Olson, H. (1976). The use of humor in psychotherapy. *Individual Psychologist, 13(1),* 34-37.

Orfandis, M.M. (1972). Children's use of humor in psychotherapy. *Social Casework, 53,* 147-155.

Perr, I.N. (1973). The world of humor, medicine, psychiatry, and the law. *Journal of Psychiatry and the Law, 1,* 493-498.

Pirandello, L. (1965). Art of humor. *Massachusetts Review, 6,* 515-520.

Potter, S. (1951). *One-upmanship. New York: Holt.*

Priest, R.F. (1966). Election jokes: The effects of reference group membership. *Psychological Reports, 18,* 600-602.

Raskin, V. (1985, October). Jokes. *Psychology Today,* 34-39.

Redlich, F.D., Levine, J., & Sohler, T.P. (1951). A mirth response test. *American Journal of Orthopsychiatry, 21,* 717-734.

Ricks, J. (1969). Our fear of laughter. *Voices, 5,* 12-15.

Rinder, I.D. (1965). Note on humor as an index of minority group morale. *Phylon, 26,* 117-121.

Roberts, A.F., & Johnson, D.M. (1957). Some factors related to the perception of funniness in humor stimuli. *Journal of Social Psychology, 46,* 57-63.

Rom, P. (1971). Reflections on the "sense of humour." *International Journal of Social Psychiatry, 17,* 225-229.

Rose, G.J. (1969). "King Lear" and the use of humor in treatment. *Journal of the American Psychoanalytic Association, 17,* 927-940.

Rosen, V. (1963). Varieties of comic caricature, and their relationship to obsessive compulsive phenomena. *Journal of the American Psychoanalytic Association, 11,* 704-724.

Rosenheim, E., & Golan, G. (1986). Patients' reactions to humorous interventions in psychotherapy. *American Journal of Psychotherapy, 40(1),* 110-124.

Rosten, L.C. (1968). *The joys of Yiddish.* New York: McGraw-Hill.

Rosenthal, H.R. (1959). The final dream: A criterion for the termination of therapy. In K.A. Adler & D. Deutsch (Eds.), *Essays in Individual Psychology,* (pp. 400-409). New York: Grove Press.

Rovit, E. (1967). Jewish humor and American life. *American Scholar, 12(1),* 7-9.

Rubin, D.E. (1972). Conversation with the author of *I Never Promised You a Rose Garden. Psychoanalytic Review, 59,* 201-215.

Rule, W.R. (1977). Increasing self-modeled humor. *Rational Living, 12(1),* 7-9.

Rycroft, C. (1969, April 10). What's so funny? Rationale of the dirty joke: An analysis of sexual humor. *New York Times Review of Books, 12,* 24-25.

Schmidt, H.E., & Williams, D.I. (1971). The evolution of theories of humor. *Journal of Behavioral Science, 1,* 95-106.

Schwartz, M.B. (1981). Receiving the message. *Voices, 16(4),* 79.

Seagull, A.A. (1966). Must the deeply disturbed have long-term treatment? *Psychotherapy, 3,* 36-42.

Shaw, F.J. (1960). Laughter, paradigm of growth. *Journal of Individual Psychology, 16,* 151-157.

Shem, S. (1985). *Fine.* New York: Dell.

Shoben, E.J., Jr. (1960). Love, loneliness, and logic. *Journal of Individual Psychology, 16,* 11-24.

Shulman, B.H., & Mosak, H.H. (1967). Various purposes of symptoms. *Journal of Individual Psychology, 23,* 79-87.

Singer, D.L., & Berkowitz, L. (1972). Differing "creativities" in the wit and the clown. *Perceptual and Motor Skills, 35,* 3-6.

Smith, E.E., & White, H.L. (1965). Wit, creativity, and sarcasm. *Journal of Applied Psychology, 49,* 131-134.

Sroufe, L.A., & Wunsch, J.P. (1972). The development of laughter in the first year of life. *Child Development, 43,* 1326-1344.

Stendhal. (1924). *Du rire.* Paris: Calmann-Levy.

Stephenson, R.M. (1951). Conflict and control functions of humor. *American Journal of Sociology, 56,* 569-574.

Stylites, S. (1950, March 8). We are not amused. *Christian Century, 67,* 297.

Sykes, A.J.M. (1966). Joking relationships in an industrial setting. *American Anthropologist, 68,* 188-193.

Treadwell, Y. (1967). Bibliography of empirical studies of wit and humor. *Psychological Reports, 20,* 1079-1083.

Treadwell, Y. (1970). Humor and creativity. *Psychological Reports, 26,* 55-58.

Ullman, L.P., & Lim, D.T. (1962). Case history material as a source of the identification of patterns of response to emotional stimuli in the study of humor. *Journal of Consulting Psychology, 26,* 221-225.

Van Dusen, W. (1961). The phenomenology of a schizophrenic experience. *Journal of Individual Psychology, 17,* 80-92.

Van Lawick-Goodall, J. (1968). A preliminary report on expressive movements and communication in the Gombe Stream chimpanzees. In P.C. Jay (Ed.), *Primates* (pp. 313-374). New York: Holt.

Weiner, I. B. (1975). *Principles of psychotherapy.* New York: John Wiley.

Weinstein, M., & Goodman, J. (1980). *Playfair*. San Luis Obispo: Impact.

Wexberg, E. (1929). *Individual Psychology*. London: Allen & Unwin.

Wieck, D. (1967). Funny things. *Journal of Aesthetics and Art Criticism, 25,* 437-447.

Williams, C., & Cole, D.L. (1964). The influence of experimentally induced inadequacy feelings upon the appreciation of humor. *Journal of Social Psychology, 53,* 113-117.

Wolfe, W.B. (1932). *How to be happy though human*. London: Routledge & Kegan Paul.

Wolff, H.A., Smith, C.E., & Murray, H.A. (1934). The psychology of humor. *Journal of Abnormal and Social Psychology, 28,* 341-365.

Wolpe, J. (1958). *Psychotherapy by reciprocal inhibition*. Stanford, CA: Stanford University Press.

Worthen, R., & O'Connell, W.E. (1969). Social interest and humor. *International Journal of Social Psychiatry, 15,* 179-188.

Yorukoglu, A. (1974). Children's favorite jokes and their relation to emotional conflicts. *Journal of the American Academy of Child Psychiatry, 13,* 677-690.

Young, R.D., & Frye, M. (1966). Some are laughing; some are not: Why? *Psychological Reports, 18,* 747-754.

Zijderveld, A. (1968). Jokes and their relation to social reality. *Social Research, 35,* 286-311.

Zillmann, D., & Cantor, J.R. (1972). Directionality of transitory dominance as a communication variable affecting humor appreciation. *Journal of Personality and Social Psychology, 24,* 191-198.

Zuk, G. (1964). A further study of laughter in family therapy. *Family Process, 3,* 77-89.

Zuk, G. (1966). On the theory and pathology of laughter in psychotherapy. *Psychotherapy, 3,* 97-101.

Zwerling, I. (1955). The favorite joke in diagnostic and therapeutic interviewing. *Psychoanalytic Quarterly, 24,* 104-114.

INDEX

Dickens, C. 58
Double meaning
    joke 29
Dreikurs, R. 10, 19, 21, 43, 47, 65,
    134, 135
Dreikurs, Sadie 58
Durante, Jimmy 33
Dworkin, E.S. 18, 49, 135

E

Efran, J.S. 18, 49, 135
Eibl-Eibesfeldt, I. 15, 16, 135
Ellenberger, H. 23, 135
Ellis, A. 67, 74, 75, 76, 135
Ezra, Rabbi Ben 33

F

Fadiman, C. 9, 135
Farrelly, F. 74, 135
Ferris, D.R. 49, 135
Flow experience 77
Frankl, V.E. 62, 63, 135
Freedman, D.G. 16, 135
Freud, S. 7, 17, 21, 26, 27, 28, 35,
    58, 135
Fried, E. 70, 135
Fromm, E. 27, 135
Frye, M. 9, 14, 18, 142
Funny
    what makes things 3-11

G

Gallows humor 35
Gardner, R.A. 51, 135
Getzels, J.W. 49, 135
Gifts
    humor 65
Gilbert, William S. 51
Goethe 43
Golan, G. 45, 140
Goldstein, J.H. 4, 18, 72, 135, 137, 138

Gondor, Lily 74
Goodchilds, J.D. 48, 72, 136
Goodman, J. 15, 142
Goodrich, A.T. 9, 136
Goodrich, D.W. 9, 136
Graham, L.R. 24, 136
Gray, D.J. 6, 136
Green, Hannah 77
Greenberg, Joanne 77
Greenberg, P.S. 30, 134
Greenwald, H. 43, 57, 136
Gregory, Dick 48
Grossman, S.A. 49, 136
Grotjahn, M. 18, 49, 70, 76, 136
Grotjahn, Martin 69, 71
Gushurst, R.S. 139

H

Hahn, J. 48, 136
Hall, G.S. 5, 136
Hassett, J. 136
Hauck, W.E. 62, 136
Henry, J. 9, 136
Hershfield, Harry 26
Hippocrates 72, 74
Holmes, Oliver Wendell 61, 62, 136
Hope, Bob 8, 33, 48
Horace 39
Houlihan, J. 136
Hrelec, E.S. 5, 138
Humor
    Black
    cartoon 67
    correlated with intelligence 49
    creating images 65
    establishing a relationship 41-3
    ethnic 8, 34
    exaggeration 64
    facilitating catharsis 56
    fun, theories, & structure 1-35
    function 23
    gallows 35
    gifts 65
    good 72
    hide behind 76
    in diagnosis 43
    in interpretation 51-9
    in psychotherapy 37-77

rabbi 22
railroad guard 123
relevance of common humanity 55
religious 90, 111
remembering 119
return merchandise 124
Rorschach examination 106
salt & pepper 30
say good night 26
schlemazel 95, 96
schlemiel 95, 96-7
second language 121
see humor
self-adulation 94-5
self-disparagement 33
sensitive individual 95
sex 92-3, 97-8, 102, 105-6, 108-9,
   110, 114, 119, 122, 123-4
sex drive 89
sexual 20
sexual content 18
shirt size 106
shit 123
sick humor 34-5
sign his name 113
snake 17
SOB 28
social interest 48
soup 29
sparrow 123
spell 26
St. Peter 104
start of 6-7
stature 112
stealing 58
structure 27-35
suicide 52, 57, 115
superiority 48
surprise 29
suspicion 48
Swedes 101-2
take trouble lightly 52
talking 121-2
Texan 127
therapy 22
transportation 31-2
two frames of reference 25
two-tracked 28
ulcers 98
undesired task 93-4
universalization 55-6

Virgin Mary 32
Volkswagen 31
warnings 116
wave 128-9
wealth 117
whiskey 122
who knows 118
wife 121, 126
zebras 124
Joke-teller 6
   cooperate with 48
   leads the listener 24
   motives 47
   personality attributes 5
   psychological factors 9
Joke-telling
   definition 10
   rules 8
Joking
   circular process 6

K

Kadis, A.L. 65, 67, 137
Kant 9
Kass, M. 47, 137
Kaye, Danny 48
Keith-Spiegel, P. 18, 137
Kelling, G.W. 18, 137
Kennedy, John F. 47
Koestler, A. 137
Kubie, L.S. 39, 40, 42, 45, 52, 65,
   73, 76, 77, 137
Kuhlman, T.L. 25, 56, 58, 75, 76, 137

L

Lathrop, D.D. 23, 48, 63, 137
Laughing at oneself
   joke 33
Laughter 13-4
   at the client 75
   canned 75
   definition 10
   gaining insight 58
   nervous 61

purposes of 22
sharing 17, 47
social act 16
support denial of reality 44
support superiority 44
use in therapy 39
wind power 62
with the client 75
Lazarsfeld, S. 66, 137
Le Shan, E. 17, 137
Leak, G.K. 18, 137
Lefcourt, H.M. 49, 137
Lenzberg, K. 5, 6, 23, 44, 56, 137
Levanthal, H. 19, 134
Levine, J. 10, 19, 25, 45, 46, 70,
  137, 140
Lifschitz, M. 65, 137
Lightstone, J. 139
Lim, D.T. 18, 141
Lowe, R. 59, 135
Ludicrous story
  joke 30-2
Lundberg, C.C. 9, 138

M

Manaster, G.J. 57, 58, 65, 74, 138
Marcus, N.N. 39, 41, 138
Martineau, W.H. 9, 34, 138
Marx Brothers 15
Marx, Groucho 30, 55
Masculinity 64
McGee, Fibber 75
McGhee, P.E. 7, 18, 24, 72, 136, 137,
  138
McReynolds, P. 70, 134
Mead, G.H. 19, 138
Meerloo, J.A.M. 69, 138
Mettee, D.R. 5, 20, 138
Mindess, H. 5, 43, 56, 64, 69, 133, 138
Moody, R.A., Jr. 6, 10, 34, 46, 63, 67,
  76, 138
Morgan, Henry 25
Mosak, B. 65, 139
Mosak, H.H. 10, 21, 42, 43, 44, 45, 47,
  52, 54, 56, 63, 64, 65, 69, 74, 135,
  137, 138, 139, 141
Murphy, B. 9, 139
Murray, H.A. 9, 142

N

Names
  humor 65
Narboe, N. 42, 73, 74, 139
Nietszche 63
Nikelly, A.G. 48, 139
Nixon, R 6
Nosanchuk, T.A. 139
Nothing sacred
  joke 32-3

O

O'Connell, W.E. 7, 9, 18, 35, 46, 47,
  48, 49, 57, 64, 139, 142
Olson, H. 69, 139
Orfandis, M.M. 49, 139
Overholt, B.J. 57, 58, 65, 74, 138

P

Painter, G. 57, 58, 65, 74, 138
Perr, I.N. 139
Peterson, P. 139
Phillips, K.S. 42, 139
Pirandello, L. 48, 140
Plato 9
Pollio, H.R. 9, 139
Polster, Erv 73, 74
Potter, S. 9, 45, 140
Priest, R.F. 6, 140
Puns 25

R

Rabelais 62
Rakusin, J. 10, 45, 137
Raskin, V. 13, 140
Redlich, F.C. 19, 25, 45, 46, 70, 137
Relationship
  establishing 41-3
Rickles, Don 75

native gift 76
trained 76
Therapy
friendship 62
Thomas, Danny 53
Thomas, J.W. 62, 136
Treadwell, Y. 4, 9, 141
Treatment
harming 74
Truman, Harry S. 35

U

Ullman, L.P. 18, 141

V

Van Dusen, W. 68, 141
Van Lawick-Goodall, J. 14, 141

W

Weiner, I.B. 141
Weinstein, M. 15, 142

Wexberg, E. 62, 142
White, H.L. 46, 48, 49, 70, 141
Wieck, D. 16, 142
Wilkins, P.C. 5, 20, 138
Williams, C. 18, 20, 142
Williams, D.I. v, 140
Winick, C. 67, 137
Wits
natural 5
Wolfe, W.B. 20, 47, 49, 63, 142
Wolff, H.A. 9, 142
Wolpe, J. 62, 142
Worthen, R. 48, 142
Wunsch, J.P. 16, 141

Y

Yorukoglu, A. 49, 142
Young, R.D. 9, 14, 18, 142

Z

Zijderveld, A. 9, 142
Zillmann, D. 9, 142
Zuk, G. 21, 45, 49, 142
Zwerling, I. 49, 142

Harold H. Mosak

Harold H. Mosak, Ph.D., is a clinical psychologist in the private practice of psychotherapy in Chicago for almost four decades. He is currently Chairman of the Board of the Alfred Adler Institute of Chicago where he is also on the faculty. Carl Rogers was his first teacher in psychotherapy at the University of Chicago where Dr. Mosak gained his doctorate in 1950. Concurrently he was in the first class of Veterans Administration interns where almost all of his training and supervision was psychoanalytically-oriented. After receiving his doctorate, he was assigned to the Veterans Administration Mental Health Clinic in Denver where his training and supervision were conducted by the Adolf Meyer

psychobiologists led by Franklin Ebaugh. In 1951 he joined in Adlerian practice with Rudolf Dreikurs and Bernard Shulman.

Adlerian psychology has a long tradition of joke-telling and story-telling which fit well with Dr. Mosak's background. Beginning with Adler, the major Adlerian psychotherapists have possessed the "gift" for telling a good story. When they have had occasion to meet, Adlerians like "Buzz" O'Connell, Bob Powers, Leo Gold, Bernie Shulman, and Mosak have spent a fun evening exchanging jokes. In his early religious training Dr. Mosak was exposed to the story, the example, the parable—illustrations which helped make a point better than explanation might. His interest in humor was furthered through his gravitation toward friends who, among other things, shared his love for the joke. (One of these, David Roth, M.D., went on to become a Freudian analyst.)

Given Elijah's criterion, Dr. Mosak still pursues the goal of gaining "a share in the world to come."